MS Excel Interview Questions

By: Terry Sanchez-Clark

MS Excel Interview Questions

ISBN: 978-1-60332-033-7

Table of Contents

I. Introduction

Microsoft Excel (full name Microsoft Office Excel) is a spreadsheet program written and distributed by Microsoft for computers using the Microsoft Windows operating system and for Apple Macintosh computers. It features an intuitive interface and capable calculation and graphing tools, which, along with aggressive marketing, have made Excel one of the most popular microcomputer applications to date. It is overwhelmingly the dominant spreadsheet application available for these platforms and has been so since version 5 in 1993, due to its bundling as part of Microsoft Office.

History:

Microsoft originally marketed a spreadsheet program called Multiplan in 1982, which was very popular on CP/M systems, but on MS-DOS systems it lost popularity to Lotus 1-2-3. This promoted development of a new spreadsheet called Excel which started with the intention to, in the words of Doug Klunder, "do everything 1-2-3 does and do it better". The first version of Excel was released for the Mac in 1985 and the first Windows version (numbered 2.0 to line-up with the Mac and bundled with a run-time Windows environment) was released in November 1987. Lotus was slow to bring 1-2-3 to Windows and by 1988 Excel had started to outsell 1-2-3 and helped Microsoft achieve the position of leading PC software developer. Dethroning the king of the software world solidified Microsoft as a valid competitor and showed its future of developing graphical software. Microsoft pushed its advantage with regular new releases, every two years or so. The current version for the Windows platform is Excel 12, also called Microsoft Office Excel 2007. The current version for the Mac OS X platform is Microsoft Excel 2004.

Early in its life Excel became the target of a trademark lawsuit by another company already selling a software package named "Excel" in the finance industry. As the result of the dispute Microsoft was required to refer to the program as "Microsoft Excel" in all of its formal press releases and legal documents. However, over time this practice has been ignored, and Microsoft cleared up the issue permanently when they purchased the trademark to the other program. Microsoft also encouraged the use of the letters XL as shorthand for the program; while this is no longer common, the program's icon on Windows still consists of a stylized combination of the two letters, and the file extension of the default Excel format is .xls.

Excel offers many user interface tweaks over the earliest electronic spreadsheets; however, the essence remains the same as in the original spreadsheet, VisiCalc: the cells are organized in rows and columns, and contain data or formulas with relative or absolute references to other cells.

Excel was the first spreadsheet that allowed the user to define the appearance of spreadsheets (fonts, character attributes and cell appearance). It also introduced intelligent cell recomputation, where only cells dependent on the cell being modified are updated (previous spreadsheet programs recomputed everything all the time or waited for a specific user command). Excel has extensive graphing capabilities.

When first bundled into Microsoft Office in 1993, Microsoft Word and Microsoft PowerPoint had their GUIs redesigned for consistency with Excel, the killer app on the PC at the time.

Since 1993, Excel has included Visual Basic for Applications (VBA), a programming language based on Visual Basic which adds the ability to automate tasks in Excel and to provide user defined functions (UDF) for use in worksheets. VBA is a powerful addition to the application which, in later versions, includes a fully featured integrated development environment (IDE). Macro recording can produce VBA code replicating user actions, thus allowing simple automation of regular tasks. VBA allows the creation of forms and in-worksheet controls to communicate with the user. The language supports use (but not creation) of ActiveX (COM) DLL's; later versions add support for class modules allowing the use of basic object-oriented programming techniques.

The automation functionality provided by VBA has caused Excel to become a target for macro viruses. This was a serious problem in the corporate world until antivirus products began to detect these viruses. Microsoft belatedly took steps to prevent the misuse by adding the ability to disable macros completely, to enable macros when opening a workbook or to trust all macros signed using a trusted certificate.

Versions 5.0 to 9.0 of Excel contain various Easter eggs, although since version 10 Microsoft has taken measures to eliminate such undocumented features from their products.

Versions:

Versions for Microsoft Windows include:

* 1987 Excel 2.0 for Windows
* 1990 Excel 3.0
* 1992 Excel 4.0
* 1993 Excel 5.0 (Office 4.2 & 4.3, also a 32-bit version for Windows NT only)
* 1995 Excel 7.0 (Office '95)
* 1997 Excel 8.0 (Office '97)
* 1999 Excel 9.0 (Office 2000)
* 2001 Excel 10.0 (Office XP)
* 2003 Excel 11.0 (Office 2003)
* 2007 Excel 12.0 (Office 2007, Now released to manufacturers. Available freely to Technet and MSDN subscribers.)
* Notice: There is no Excel 1.0, in order to avoid confusion with Apple versions.
* Notice: There is no Excel 6.0, because it was launched with Word 7. All the Office 95 products have OLE 2 capacity - moving data automatically from various programmes - and Excel 7 should show that it was contemporary with Word 7.

Versions for the Apple Macintosh include:

* 1985 Excel 1.0
* 1988 Excel 1.5
* 1989 Excel 2.2
* 1990 Excel 3.0
* 1992 Excel 4.0
* 1993 Excel 5.0
* 1998 Excel 8.0 (Office '98)
* 2000 Excel 9.0 (Office 2001)
* 2001 Excel 10.0 (Office v. X)
* 2004 Excel 11.0 (Office 2004)

Versions for OS/2 include:

* 1989 Excel 2.2
* 1991 Excel 3.0

File formats:

Microsoft Excel has traditionally used a proprietary binary file format called Binary Interchange File Format (BIFF). Microsoft Excel 2002 and subsequent versions also support an XML format called "XML Spreadsheet" ("XMLSS") [1], although this format is not able to encode VBA macros. Microsoft Excel 2007 additionally supports the Office Open XML format. As of 2007, various efforts are underway to allow Microsoft Excel to manipulate OpenDocument files. In addition, most versions of Microsoft Excel are able to read CSV, DBF, SYLK, and other legacy formats.

Criticism:

The statistical accuracy of Excel has been criticized, as has the lack of certain statistical tools. Excel proponents have pointed out that this is an edge case and the relatively few users who would be affected by these flaws know of them and have workarounds and alternatives.

Excel incorrectly assumes that 1900 is a leap year. The bug originated from Lotus 1-2-3, and was implemented in Excel for the purpose of backward compatibility. This legacy has later been carried over into Office Open XML file format. Excel also supports the second date format based on year 1904 epoch.

II. Excel Programming Questions and Answers

Question 1: ScreenUpdating function not working

I'm using Office 2003 on Win XP Pro SP2, Dell PC. I have the following VBA script in a spreadsheet, and I want to hide all the activity; but the ScreenUpdating function doesn't seem to be hiding anything as tons of stuff still shows on screen. I did the following:

```
-----------------------------------------

Private Sub cmdApp_Click()

' Turn off Screen Updating
Application.ScreenUpdating = False

' Unprotect the worksheet
Excel.SendKeys ("%(t)")
Excel.SendKeys ("p")
Excel.SendKeys ("p")
Excel.SendKeys ("excel")
Excel.SendKeys ("{ENTER}")

' Goto Cell A22
Excel.SendKeys ("{F5}")
Excel.SendKeys ("{DELETE}")
Excel.SendKeys ("A22")
Excel.SendKeys ("{ENTER}")

' Select current row and next 7 rows
Excel.SendKeys ("+({DOWN 7})")

' Insert a bunch of rows
Excel.SendKeys ("%(i)")
Excel.SendKeys ("r")

' Move cursor down 1 row
Excel.SendKeys ("{DOWN}")

' Format row height then go to next row
Excel.SendKeys ("%(o)re12.75{ENTER}")
```

```
Excel.SendKeys ("{DOWN}")

' Format row height then go to next row
Excel.SendKeys ("%(o)re3.75{ENTER}")
Excel.SendKeys ("{DOWN}")

' Format row height then go to next row
Excel.SendKeys ("%(o)re12.75{ENTER}")
Excel.SendKeys ("{DOWN}")

' Format row height then go to next row
Excel.SendKeys ("%(o)re3.75{ENTER}")
Excel.SendKeys ("{DOWN}")

' Format row height then go to next row
Excel.SendKeys ("%(o)re12.75{ENTER}")
Excel.SendKeys ("{DOWN}")

' Format row height then go to next row
Excel.SendKeys ("%(o)re12.75{ENTER}")
Excel.SendKeys ("{DOWN}")

' Format row height then go to next row
Excel.SendKeys ("%(o)re2.50{ENTER}")
Excel.SendKeys ("{DOWN}")

' Insert another row
Excel.SendKeys ("%(i)")
Excel.SendKeys ("r")

' Move cursor two cells to the right
Excel.SendKeys ("{RIGHT 2}")

' Select 6 columns wide (blank row that was just inserted)
Excel.SendKeys ("+({RIGHT 6})")

' Format cell pattern to be solid black
Excel.SendKeys ("%(o)ebp{TAB}{DOWN}{ENTER}{TAB
2}{ENTER}")

' Go down two rows
Excel.SendKeys ("{DOWN 2}")
```

```
' Select 3 columns and 4 rows
Excel.SendKeys ("+({RIGHT 3}{DOWN 4})")

' Copy selected rows
Excel.SendKeys ("^(c)")

' Move curser up 9 rows
Excel.SendKeys ("{UP 9}")

' Paste rows from previous copy then ESC out of copy sequence
Excel.SendKeys ("^(v)")
Excel.SendKeys ("{ESC}")

' Move right one cell, delete its contents
Excel.SendKeys ("{RIGHT}")
Excel.SendKeys ("{DELETE}")

' Move right two cells, delete its contents
Excel.SendKeys ("{RIGHT 2}")
Excel.SendKeys ("{DELETE}")

' Move down 2 and left 1 cell, delete its contents
Excel.SendKeys ("{DOWN 2}{LEFT}{DELETE}")

' Move down 2 cells, delete its contents
Excel.SendKeys ("{DOWN 2}{DELETE}")

' Move up 4 cells and left 1 cell
Excel.SendKeys ("{UP 4}{LEFT}")

' Re-protect the worksheet
Excel.SendKeys ("%(t)pp")
Excel.SendKeys ("excel")
Excel.SendKeys ("{ENTER}")
Excel.SendKeys ("excel")
Excel.SendKeys ("{ENTER}")

' Turn Screen Updating back on
Application.ScreenUpdating = True
```

Can you help me clear this problem?

A: You can use the following. You might need to replace the values so the code will suit your needs.

```
Option Explicit
Private Sub cmdApp_Click()

'[Removed Dim statement (for iRows) since For/Next loop was
removed]
'Turn off Screen Updating
Application.ScreenUpdating = False

'Unprotect the worksheet
With ActiveSheet
.Unprotect Password:="excel"

'Goto Cell A22
'Insert a bunch of rows
'[I modified the Resize property]
.Range("a22").Resize(9, 1).EntireRow.Insert

'[Removed the For/Next loop and set specific row references]
.Rows(23).RowHeight = 12.75
.Rows(24).RowHeight = 3.75
.Rows(25).RowHeight = 12.75
.Rows(26).RowHeight = 3.75
.Rows(27).RowHeight = 12.75
.Rows(28).RowHeight = 12.75
.Rows(29).RowHeight = 2.25
.Rows(30).RowHeight = 2.25
.Rows(31).RowHeight = 4.5

'[Modified the ranges and removed the 'offset' methods]
.Range("C30").Resize(1, 7).Interior.ColorIndex = 1
.Range("C32").Resize(6, 7).Copy Destination:=.Range("C23")

Application.CutCopyMode = False

'[Because these were merged cells it kept generating an error,
' so I modified the ranges to accommodate the merges.]
.Range("D23:E23").ClearContents
.Range("G23:I23").ClearContents
.Range("D25:F25").ClearContents
.Range("D27:I28").ClearContents
```

```
.Range("D23:E23").Select

'Re-protect the worksheet
.Protect Password:="excel"

End With

'Turn Screen Updating back on
Application.ScreenUpdating = True

End Sub
Private Sub cmdSubmit_Click()
Excel.SendKeys ("%(f)")
Excel.SendKeys ("da")
```

Question 2: Excel menu bar has dissapeared

The menu bar (File, Edit, View, etc.) has dissapeared in my Excel 2003. I tried reinstalling and have checked the knowledge base but can't find out how to get it to reappear.

Can you help me solve this?

A: If any toolbars or menubars are visible, right click on a blank area of the menu bar and select 'customize'. Then select worksheet menu bar in the first tab and click on it so it is selected. Close the dialog box.

If you are conversant in VBA, go to the immediate window in the VBE and type:

Application.CommandBars("Worksheet Menu Bar").Enabled = True
then
Application.CommandBars("Worksheet Menu Bar").Visible = True

If you find that they disappear again (or that you missed some), you just need to reset that worksheet menu bar.

Tools > customize > toolbars tab
Select worksheet Menu bar then click the reset button.

Question 3: How to make a formula cell dynamically display in Excel Worksheet Functions

There is a simple formula =sum(A1:A10).

If any of the cell in range A1:A10 is changed, how do you make the cell which contain the formula display the change?

A: You will need to access Tools > Options > Calculation:

Make sure it says "Automatic", not "Manual".

Also, if calculation is set to manual you can recalculate at any time by pressing F9.

Question 4 : Making several Excel Applications Visible

Is it possible to write a sub that would make visible (Excel.Visible=True) various instances of Excel applications that are currently running invisible?

I'm debugging a VB program that opens a new Excel application and keeps it invisible (Excel.Visible-False) while processing data, and then closes it (Excel.Quit). As I am debugging it, I often interrupt the program (because of exceptions, etc.) before it quits Excel, and I subsequently find in the Task Manager. Numerous Excel applications are running, but they are all invisible. I can't look at them or close them easily.

I know you can access one Excel application using GetObject ("Excel.Application"), but is there a way to loop through all of the Excel applications running to make each of them visible?

I can see how many are running using Diagnostics.Process.GetProcessesByName, but I can't figure out how to make all of them visible. I'm not creating an array of Excel applications. I'm simply running a program that starts with, for example:

```
Dim Exc as new Excel.Application
Exc.Visible=False
... (code here) ...
Exc.Quit
```

Is there a solution for this?

A: Here's a sample to show all Excel windows using EnumWindows and callback:

Option Explicit

```
Public Declare Function EnumWindows Lib "user32"
(ByVal lpEnumFunc As Long,
ByVal lParam As Long) As Long
Public Declare Function IsWindowVisible Lib "user32"
(ByVal hwnd As Long)
```

```
As Long
Public Declare Function GetWindowText Lib "user32"
Alias "GetWindowTextA"
(ByVal hwnd As Long, ByVal lpString As String, ByVal
cch As Long) As Long
Public Declare Function GetWindowTextLength Lib
"user32" Alias
"GetWindowTextLengthA" (ByVal hwnd As Long) As Long
Public Declare Function BringWindowToTop Lib "user32"
(ByVal hwnd As Long)
As Long
Public Declare Function SetForegroundWindow Lib
"user32" (ByVal hwnd As
Long) As Long
Public Declare Function GetClassName Lib "user32"
Alias "GetClassNameA"
(ByVal hwnd As Long, ByVal lpClassName As String,
ByVal nMaxCount As Long)
As Long
Public Declare Function ShowWindow Lib "user32.dll"
(ByVal hwnd As Long,
ByVal nCmdShow As Long) As Long

Public Const SW_SHOW As Long = 5
Public Const SW_SHOWDEFAULT As Long = 10
Public Const SW_SHOWMAXIMIZED As Long = 3
Public Const SW_SHOWMINIMIZED As Long = 2
Public Const SW_SHOWMINNOACTIVE As Long = 7
Public Const SW_SHOWNA As Long = 8
Public Const SW_SHOWNOACTIVATE As Long = 4
Public Const SW_SHOWNORMAL As Long = 1


Public Function EnumWindowsProc(ByVal hwnd As Long,
ByVal lParam As Long)
As Long
If ClassName(hwnd) = "XLMAIN" Then
ShowWindow hwnd, SW_SHOWNORMAL
End If

EnumWindowsProc = 1 ' return 0 will stop enumerating
End Function

Sub Main()
EnumWindows AddressOf EnumWindowsProc, ByVal 0&
End Sub
```

```
Public Function WindowTitle(ByVal lHwnd As Long) As
String
Dim lLen As Long
Dim sBuf As String

lLen = GetWindowTextLength(lHwnd)
If (lLen > 0) Then
sBuf = String$(lLen + 1, 0)
lLen = GetWindowText(lHwnd, sBuf, lLen + 1)
WindowTitle = Left$(sBuf, lLen)
End If
End Function

Public Function ClassName(ByVal lHwnd As Long) As
String
Dim lLen As Long
Dim sBuf As String
lLen = 260
sBuf = String$(lLen, 0)
lLen = GetClassName(lHwnd, sBuf, lLen)
If (lLen <> 0) Then
ClassName = Left$(sBuf, lLen)
End If
End Function
```

Question 5: Export to Excel

How do I check if Excel is open before I run my code?

I have a code that transfers data from Access to Excel. I use Excel.Application object as I have to do complex manipulation of the data. If the Excel application is already open and modified, I get Error 91.

I would also like to export my data without having to close the open Excel application. How do I do this?

A: Here is the proper way to open an instance of Excel depending on whether or not Excel is already running:

```
On Error Resume Next ' Defer error trapping.
Set xlApp = GetObject(, "Excel.Application")
If Err.Number <> 0 Then
blnExcelWasNotRunning = True
Set xlApp = CreateObject("excel.application")
Else
DetectExcel
End If
Err.Clear ' Clear Err object in case error occurred.
```

This is the sub called in the code above.

```
Sub DetectExcel()
' Procedure dectects a running Excel and registers
it.
Const WM_USER = 1024
Dim hWnd As Long
' If Excel is running this API call returns its
handle.
hWnd = FindWindow("XLMAIN", 0)
If hWnd = 0 Then ' 0 means Excel not running.
Exit Sub
Else
' Excel is running so use the SendMessage API
' function to enter it in the Running Object Table.
SendMessage hWnd, WM_USER + 18, 0, 0
End If
```

```
End Sub
```

As to not closing the Excel application, sorry, but you really have to; otherwise, you will leave an instance of Excel running that you don't want. It will cause problems if you run your code then try to open any other Excel file in Windows. It will hang up on you. In this case, you will find Excel.exe listed in the Processes tab of Task Manager.

If you use the code above to open excel, this code will only destroy the instance of Excel if it had to create a new instance.

```
xlBook.Close
If blnExcelWasNotRunning = True Then
xlApp.Quit
Else
xlApp.DisplayAlerts = True
xlApp.Interactive = True
xlApp.ScreenUpdating = True
End If
Set xlSheet = Nothing
Set xlBook = Nothing
Set xlApp = Nothing
```

Question 6: Excel Automation

I am attempting to automate the opening of Excel from Access.
In order for Excel to do what I need, I have to install an addin.
The problem that I got is the addin is opening another instance
of Excel. After Excel is opened and the addin installed, I then
need to calculate the data on Excel and import the data into
Access. I would like this to happen without any user input.

Is this task possible?

Here is the code I used:

```
Dim objXL As Object
Set objXL = CreateObject("Excel.Application")
objXL.Workbooks.Open (objXL.LibraryPath &
"\AtData.XLA") '.RunAutoMacros 1
objXL.Workbooks.Open "C:\AlkyLabData.xls"
objXL.Visible = False

DoCmd.TransferSpreadsheet , , "TestingImportData2",
"C:\AlkyLabData.xls", True

Me.Requery
DoCmd.GoToRecord , , acLast
objXL.Quit
Set objXL = Nothing
```

A: You have to be very careful with Excel objects and fully
qualify each reference. Access will create another instance if it
can't figure out which object another object belongs to. This will
cause problems with Excel processes still running. You will see
them on the 'Processes' pane of Task Manager, not the
Application pane.

Try this:

Dim objXL As Object
Dim xlBook1 as Object
Dim xlBook2 as Object
Set objXL = CreateObject("Excel.Application")
Set xlBook1 = objXL.Workbooks.Open (objXL.LibraryPath
& "\AtData.XLA") '.RunAutoMacros 1

```
Set XlBook2 = objXL.Workbooks.Open "C:\AlkyLabData.xls"
objXL.Visible = False
xlbook1.Close
xlbook2.Close
objXL.Quit
Set objXL = Nothing
Set xlBook1 = Nothing
Set xlBook2 = Nothing

DoCmd.TransferSpreadsheet , , "TestingImportData2",
"C:\AlkyLabData.xls", True

Me.Requery
DoCmd.GoToRecord , , acLast
```

Also, copied from VB Editor Help is some code that makes this straightforward. Copy this into a standard module. For example, I call mine,

modExcelRoutines

```
Option Compare Database
Option Explicit

' Declare necessary API routines:
Declare Function FindWindow Lib "user32" Alias _
"FindWindowA" (ByVal lpClassName As String, _
ByVal lpWindowName As Long) As Long

Declare Function SendMessage Lib "user32" Alias _
"SendMessageA" (ByVal hWnd As Long, ByVal wMsg As Long, _
ByVal wParam As Long, _
ByVal lParam As Long) As Long

Sub GetExcel()
Dim MyXL As Object ' Variable to hold reference
' to Microsoft Excel.
Dim ExcelWasNotRunning As Boolean ' Flag for final release.

' Test to see if there is a copy of Microsoft Excel already running.
On Error Resume Next ' Defer error trapping. ' Getobject
function called without the first argument returns a  reference to
```

an instance of the application. If the application isn't ' running, an error occurs.

```
Set MyXL = GetObject(, "Excel.Application")
If Err.Number <> 0 Then ExcelWasNotRunning = True
Err.Clear ' Clear Err object in case error occurred.

' Check for Microsoft Excel. If Microsoft Excel is running,
' enter it into the Running Object table.
DetectExcel

' Set the object variable to reference the file you want to see.
Set MyXL = GetObject("c:\vb4\MYTEST.XLS")

' Show Microsoft Excel through its Application property. Then
' show the actual window containing the file using the Windows
' collection of the MyXL object reference.
MyXL.Application.Visible = True
MyXL.Parent.Windows(1).Visible = True
' Do manipulations of your file here.
' ...
' If this copy of Microsoft Excel was not running when you
' started, close it using the Application property's Quit method.
' Note that when you try to quit Microsoft Excel, the
' title bar blinks and a message is displayed asking if you
' want to save any loaded files.
If ExcelWasNotRunning = True Then
MyXL.Application.Quit
End If

Set MyXL = Nothing ' Release reference to the
' application and spreadsheet.
End Sub

Sub DetectExcel()
' Procedure dectects a running Excel and registers it.
Const WM_USER = 1024
Dim hWnd As Long
' If Excel i running this API call returns its handle.
hWnd = FindWindow("XLMAIN", 0)
If hWnd = 0 Then ' 0 means Excel not running.
Exit Sub
Else
```

' Excel is running so use the SendMessage API
' function to enter it in the Running Object Table.
SendMessage hWnd, WM_USER + 18, 0, 0
End If

End Sub

Question 7: Write a macro in Excel Programming

I want to write a macro that copies any numbers in a cell & appends those numbers proceeded by a "." to the contents of another cell in the same row.

For example:

r1c1 r1c2

Boxholder PO Boxholder 123

The macro would copy the number value of r1c2 (123) and append the contents of r1c1 preceded by a period.

Results desired:

Boxholder.123 PO Boxholder 123

The macro would have a control+c shortcut and would execute only once for the selected row.

Can you help me with this?

A: Most people use Column Letters instead of numbers, so most would use Option, General (tab), settings: (uncheck) R1C1 style.

In which case, your R1C1 would be A1 and the R1C2 would be B1.

So if you have a cell A1 with "ABC" and a cell B1 with "123" and you want to connect the two with a space between then, you have a concatenation of a cell, a space and a second cell, the formula might be in cell C1. For example:

A1: ABC
B1: 123
C1: =A1 & " " & B1 note the quotes enclose a single space as a text constant

You need to write a macro and from your example, you are to concatenate "Boxholder" in front of each cell with a value in a selection (specifically in a selected row). You need to assign a specific shortcut to your macro; a shortcut that nobody working with a PC would assign to a macro because Ctrl+C is specifically used to copy a selection to the clipboard in many PC applications and certainly in Excel. So Part 1 of your course working with spreadsheet formulas you skipped over, and was thrown into Part 2 programming. After this exercise, Excel's own Ctrl+C will no longer work and you will have to figure out why.

You can also try this:

Select the rows you want to work with (multiple rows are ok) and run this:

```
Option Explicit
Sub testme()

Dim myRng As Range
Dim myCell As Range
Dim iCtr As Long
Dim LastSpacePos As Long
Dim myStr As String

With ActiveSheet
Set myRng = Intersect(.Range("a:a"),
Selection.EntireRow)
End With

For Each myCell In myRng.Cells
myStr = myCell.Offset(0, 1).Value
LastSpacePos = 0
For iCtr = Len(myStr) To 1 Step -1
If Mid(myStr, iCtr, 1) = " " Then
LastSpacePos = iCtr
Exit For
End If
Next iCtr

If LastSpacePos = 0 Then
```

```
'no spaces, skip it
Else
myCell.Value = myCell.Value & "." & Mid(myStr,
LastSpacePos + 1)
End If
Next myCell
End Sub
```

And assign it to the shortcutkey of your choice.

III. VB.NET General Discussions

Question 8: Opening Excel Workbook

I tried to open an Excel Workbook from VB.NET. I used the code below:

```
'open excel document
Dim ThisApplication As New Excel._ExcelApplication
Dim wb As Excel.Workbook =
ThisApplication.Workbooks.Open("C:\ExpenseReport.xls"
)
```

I got this error:

```
An unhandled exception of type
'System.Runtime.InteropServices.COMException'
occurred in mscorlib.dll
Additional information: Member not found.
```

The section highlighed when the error pops up is: wb As Excel.Workbook = ThisApplication.Workbooks.Open("C:\ExpenseReport.xls").

I am using Excel from Office 2003. I don't want to create a new workbook, but open an existing one.
When I changed the code to:

```
'open excel document
Dim ThisApplication As Excel.Application
Dim wb As Excel.Workbook =
ThisApplication.Workbooks.Open("C:\ExpenseReport.xls"
)
```

I got this error instead:

```
An unhandled exception of type
'System.NullReferenceException' occurred in
CorporateTravelExpenseReport.exe
Additional information: Object reference not set to
an instance of an object.
```

How do I solve this?

A: When using Excel 11, you need to add:

```
Imports Microsoft.Office.Interop
```

At the very top you code, or under Option Explicit On/OptionStrict On commands. Then make sure you have a reference set to: Interop.Excel.dll then:

```
Dim xlApp As Excel.Application
Dim xlWB1 As Excel.Workbook
xlApp = New Excel.Application
xlApp.Visible = True
xlWB1 =
xlApp.Workbooks.Open("C:\DLoad\CellPhoneNumbers.xls")
'xlWB1.Close()
'xlWB1 = Nothing
'xlApp.Quit()
'xlApp = Nothing
```

IV. Excel General Questions

Question 9: Open Excel 2003 from Windows Explorer

I can't open an Excel file from Windows Explorer if Excel has not been opened first. What I see on the screen is an Excel without a spreadsheet. Clicking on any menu or button fails to work. I can only click on the Close red X to close Excel. As Excel closes, I can see the spreadsheet for just a flash.

Other Office products work as expected except this problem with Excel.

Is this a bug or is there a setting I need to do to correct this problem?

A: The problem is when double-clicking on the xls-icon (as in your Win Explorer case), that Excel opens, but not the file itself.

You will need to change your settings under 'Tools menu', then 'Options', under the 'General Tab'; you need to tick off the "ignore other applications" if it is ticked on.

Question 10: My Excel 2000 won't open

I can't get my Excel files to open. The program box comes up and the hour glass just sits there waiting. Then low resources error comes on when you try to ctrl-alt-delete.

I tried re-installing office but I still get the same result.

How do I correct this problem?

A: It is most likely that you have a corrupt toolbar file.

With Excel closed, go to this folder:

```
C:\Documents and Settings\<user name>\Application
Data\Microsoft\Excel
```

And rename the file EXCEL.XLB to something else like Excel.abc and then see if Excel will start.

Changing Excel.xlb to Excel.abc was just to keep Excel from loading it when it starts up, and to give you the ability to rename it back if the XLB was not the problem. Every time you make a change to your toolbars or menubars, Excel saves those 'customizations' (intentional or not) in your XLB file.

For some reasons, the XLB file sometimes becomes corrupted and Excel hangs when starting up. The only answer I know of is to delete or rename the XLB. If you had any intentional customizations they would have to be re-created.

It is a good practice to make a backup copy of your good XLB file just in case it goes bad. That way, you don't have to start over from scratch.

Question 11: Attach to open Excel process

Is it possible to attach to an open process and perform automation on it?

I have an application that needs to manipulate Excel files extensively. Most of the manipulation goes on with Excel application hidden. But sometimes, I need the user to edit the Excel files. Before parsing the file again, I like to check that it is not left open and potentially unsaved in an Excel application window.

I know it is not possible to run this code:

```
Dim a As Excel.Application
For Each p As Process In
Process.GetProcessesByName("Excel")
a = DirectCast(p, Excel.Application)
'Check if any of these processes:
'1) Are Hidden remnants from previous unsuccessful
automation and needs to be closed
'2) Have a specific file open that needs to be saved
before
it is read
Next
```

Is there some similar method to attach to an Excel process and get hold of it as an automation object that can be investigated? Is there any other workaround to accomplish such a thing?

In my case I would like to check whether a specific Excel file is open. I came up with the following simple function that works fine:

```
Private Function IsOpen(ByVal fileName As String) As
Boolean
Dim wb As Excel.Workbook
```

```
Try
wb = DirectCast(Marshal.BindToMoniker(fileName),
Excel.Workbook)
Return True
Catch ex As Exception
Return False
End Try
End Function
```

Is that a good way to do it, or would there be a better way that avoids throwing an exception? Do I need to do a cleanup by setting wb = Nothing?

A: If you don't need to use the variable "wb" any more in your program, you should set wb = Nothing to release the reference.

As for the question of checking whether a specific Excel file is open, I don't think the BindToMoniker method is appropriate in this case; it will open the specified file if it has not been opened yet as you have mentioned.

When we open a file with Excel, the file is opened exclusively. We can make use of this feature to check if the file has been opened already. What we need to do is to try to open the specified file. If an exception occurs, it means that the file has been opened; otherwise, the file hasn't been opened.

The following is the sample code.

```
Private Function IsOpen(ByVal filename As String) As
Boolean
Try
Dim fs As System.IO.FileStream =
System.IO.File.OpenWrite(filename)
fs.Close()
Return False
Catch ex As Exception
Return True
End Try
End Function
```

Question 12: Lost ability to open (activate) Excel files from Explorer, Outlook

I have lost the ability to open Excel files by clicking on their icon from within programs apart from Excel. For example, if I click on an Excel file icon from Explorer or Outlook, then Excel starts but the file I wanted does not open. If I use Excel to open the file there are no problems.

A: You can try this first:

Tools > Options > General, uncheck "Ignore other Applications". Exit Excel and try again.

If this doesn't work try to re-register Excel.

Close Excel first and On the Windows Taskbar

1) Start > Run "excel.exe /unregserver"(no quotes)>OK.
2) Start > Run "excel.exe /regserver"(no quotes)>OK.

Note the space between exe and /regserver.

You may have to designate a full path to excel.exe.

In that case Start>Run "C:\yourpath\excel.exe /regserver"(no quotes)>OK.

Question 13: Microsoft Excel in Microsoft works - how to open

How do I open an Excel document using Microsoft Works spreadsheet?

I do not have Microsoft Excel in my PC.

A: You need to ask the person who created the excel document to save it to a version that Works can open or you can download the free viewer (no changes allowed) from Microsoft:

There are also a large variety of free spreadsheet programs available on the Internet that will work for you:

Question 14: Generating Excel Chart from Access Form in Importing and Exporting Data

I was generating an Excel2000 Chart from an MSAccess2000 Form. When I finished viewing the chart, I could not close Excel properly. When I change the MSAccess Form data, I can no longer generate the Excel Chart. There is an instance of Excel remaining open in the background preventing the reuse of the MSAccess Form to generate a new Excel Chart.

When I try to shut down the PC, there are multiple back ground instances of Excel that have to be shut down before the PC can be shut down. I went back to the MSAccess Form and used an MSAccess command to close Excel.

```
Private Sub cmdCreateGraph_Click()
On Error GoTo cmdCreateGraph_Err
Dim rstData As ADODB.Recordset
Dim rstCount As ADODB.Recordset
Dim fld As ADODB.Field
Dim rng As Excel.Range
Dim objWS As Excel.Worksheet
Dim intRowCount As Integer
Dim intColCount As Integer


'Display Hourglass
'DoCmd.Hourglass True
Set rstData = New ADODB.Recordset
rstData.ActiveConnection = CurrentProject.Connection
Set rstCount = New ADODB.Recordset
rstCount.ActiveConnection = CurrentProject.Connection


'Attempt to create Recordset and launch Excel
If CreateRecordset(rstData, rstCount,
"qrySalesByCountry") Then
If CreateExcelObj() Then
gobjExcel.Workbooks.Add
Set objWS = gobjExcel.ActiveSheet
intRowCount = 1
intColCount = 1
'Loop though Fields collection using field names
'as column headings
```

```
For Each fld In rstData.Fields
If fld.Type <> adLongVarBinary Then
objWS.Cells(1, intColCount).Value = fld.Name
intColCount = intColCount + 1
End If
Next fld
'Send Recordset to Excel
objWS.Range("A1").CopyFromRecordset rstData, 500


'Format Data
With gobjExcel
.Columns("A:B").Select
.Columns("A:B").EntireColumn.AutoFit
.Range("A1").Select
.ActiveCell.CurrentRegion.Select
Set rng = .Selection
.Selection.NumberFormat = "$#,##0.00"
'Add a Chart Object
.ActiveSheet.ChartObjects.Add(135.75, 14.25, 607.75,
301).Select

'''''''''''''''''''''''''''''''''''''''''''''''''''''''
'''''''''''''''''''''''''''''''''''''''
ActiveChart.ChartType = xlColumnClustered
ActiveChart.SetSourceData
Source:=Sheets("Sheet1").Range("A1:B21"), PlotBy _
:=xlColumns
ActiveChart.Location Where:=xlLocationAsNewSheet
With ActiveChart
.HasTitle = True
.ChartTitle.Characters.Text = "Corrosion Rate"
.Axes(xlCategory, xlPrimary).HasTitle = False
.Axes(xlValue, xlPrimary).HasTitle = True
.Axes(xlValue, xlPrimary).AxisTitle.Characters.Text =
_
"Corrosion Rate (mpy)"
End With
ActiveChart.HasLegend = False
ActiveChart.HasDataTable = False '''

'''''''''''''''''''''''''''''''''''''''''''''''''''''''
'''''''''''''''''''''''''''''''''''
'Make Excel Visible
.Visible = True
End With
Else
MsgBox "Excel Not Successfully Launched"
```

```
End If
Else
MsgBox "Too Many Records to Send to Excel"
End If
DoCmd.Hourglass False

cmdCreateGraph_Exit:
Set rstData = Nothing
Set rstCount = Nothing
Set fld = Nothing
Set rng = Nothing
Set objWS = Nothing
DoCmd.Hourglass False
Exit Sub

cmdCreateGraph_Err:
MsgBox "Error # " & Err.Number & ": " &
Err.Description
Resume cmdCreateGraph_Exit
End Sub

'Close Excel from the MSAccess Form using this
cmd_click
Private Sub Command3_Click()
CloseExcel
End Sub
```

A: You haven't shown what your CreateExcelObj() function does; but from your description of its behavior, it creates a new instance of Excel and points gobjExcel at it, thus leaving any previous instances isolated in the background.

To avoid this, use something like this air code instead:

```
Function GetExcelApplication() As Object
Dim objXL As Excel.Application
On Error Resume Next
'Try to grab an existing instance of Excel
Set objXL = GetObject(,"Excel.Application")
If objXL Is Nothing Then
'None found, create a new one
Set objXL = CreateObject("Excel.Application")
End If
If objXL Is Nothing Then
MsgBox "Excel Not Successfully Launched"
Set GetExcelApplication = Nothing
Else
```

```
Set GetExcelApplication = objXL
End If
Set objXL = Nothing
End Function
```

And in your graphing procedure:

```
Dim objXL As Excel.Application
...
Set objXL = GetExcelApplication()
If obXL Is Nothing Then
MsgBox "Couldn't launch Excel"
Else
'go to work on objXL instead of gobjExcel

End If
```

This should avoid the creation of multiple hidden instances of
Excel. But if GetExcelApplication() creates a new instance and
cmdCreateGraph_Click()then calls its error handler before
reaching the line

```
.Visible = True
```

You will get one invisible instance left behind. To avoid this, use
something like this in the error handler:

```
If Not objXL Is Nothing Then
objXL.Visible = True
End If
```

The Excel instance will be visible for the user to dispose later.

Question 15: Importing in Excel

Is there a way to import .123 files into Excel 2007?

A: Yes. Open Office will open .123 files; you can save them in Excel format.

Question 16: Automation from Access into Excel

I generated a report on Access then I exported it to Word. Then I copied it from Word and tried to paste it into Excel. I am having problems with Excel ending its "thing". The following is my code:

How do I automate Excel to quit automatically?

A: When automating Excel, you should set a reference to every object you refer to in Excel. Then use the object references.

When quitting Excel, you must set each object reference to 'Nothing'. Not doing so can leave orphan references to Excel which prevent Excel from quitting. You may also want to defer copying of the Word selection just before you paste it into Excel.

Question 17: Automation from access into excel

I tried the following in Excel, and it works. But when I run it from access, I encountered problems.

```
MyWorkbook.Save
MySheet.Range("A2").EntireRow.Select

Do While ActiveCell.Value <> ""
ActiveCell.EntireRow.Insert
ActiveCell.Offset(2, 0).EntireRow.Select
Loop
MyWorkbook.Save
MyWorkbook.Close SaveChanges:=True
Set MySheet = Nothing
```

How do I correct this?

A: Don't use ActiveCell, Selection, UsedRange, etc. Use object references:

```
Set MyCell = MySheet.Range("A2")

Do While MyCell.Value <> ""
MyCell.EntireRow.Insert
Set MyCell = MyCell.Offset(2, 0)
Loop
```

Question 18: MsAccess and Excel versions in Office Developer Automation

I use a VBA Application in MsAccess 2003 that opens an EXCEL 2003 .xlt file. I had to install the .mdb file on another computer that has MsAcces 2003 but Excel 2002 got an error message saying "no reference found" for Excel v.3.1.

Do I have to upgrade the Excel version to 2003 or is there a way to bypass the problem and maintain the 2002 version?

A: Commonly COM application is back-compatible. That is to say, an application built with Excel 2002 will be running correctly on Excel 2003, but an application built with Excel 2003 is not sure to run on previous Excel versions.

A possible workaround is to use LateBinding

Question 19: Using Statistical Functions in Access Queries

Is there a way to use Excel's statistical functions in an Access query?

I like to generate a gamma distribution and I can do so in Excel using the GAMMADIST() function. However, it appears as though Access can't utilize these functions.

Is there something I need to do to be able to access these functions?

A: The GAMMADIST function is an Excel worksheet function; so having established a reference to Excel you need to call it in Access as follows:

Excel.WorksheetFunction.GammaDist(10,9,2,False)
or:

Excel.WorksheetFunction.GammaDist(10,9,2,True)

Rather than calling it directly, you will be better wrapping it in a VBA function:

```
Function GetGammaDist(x, alpha, beta, cumulative)

GetGammaDist = _
Excel.WorksheetFunction.GammaDist(x, alpha, beta,
cumulative)

End Function
```

Regarding your second question, you can work with Excel objects from Access using automation.

Question 20: Unable to close Excel application with macro in Macros

I used the following code in Access to open an instance of Excel to do some worksheet operations and close Excel at the end.

```
Dim appXL As Excel.Application
Set appXL = CreateObject("excel.application")
appXL.Visible = True
... code to open excel file, do some simple
operations, save file ...
appXL.Quit
Set appXL = Nothing
```

When the macro is done, it seems like Excel closed normally (gone from task bar), but in fact there's still an instance of Excel in the Process tab of Task Manager (Application tab shows no Excel).

If I run the same macro again the second time, it basically crashes at the first line after opening the spreadsheet file. I got the message:

```
Run-time error '1004': Method 'Cells' of object
'_Global' failed
```

I see 2 Excel listed in Process tab of Task Manager, with only 1 Excel in Application tab, and also 1 Excel in taskbar at the bottom of screen.

If I press the Reset button in the VBA window after running the macro, that Excel instance in Task Manager would truly exit. After that I can run the same macro a second time with no problem. That means I will need to press the Reset button each time after running the macro, if I wanted to run the same macro again without crashing. I can't expect the user to do the same thing.

I am using Office 2003. The following is my complete sub.

```
Private Sub cmdImport_Click()
```

```
Dim appXL As New Excel.Application
appXL.Visible = True

Dim strOpenFile As String
strOpenFile = appXL.GetOpenFilename("Excel Files
(*.xls), *.xls", , "Select
.xls file")

If strOpenFile = "False" Then
appXL.Quit
Exit Sub
End If

appXL.Workbooks.Open strOpenFile

Range("J:J,L:L,O:U,W:W,Z:AB,AD:AD").Select
Selection.Replace What:=" ", Replacement:="",
LookAt:=xlPart, _
SearchOrder:=xlByRows, MatchCase:=False,
SearchFormat:=False,
ReplaceFormat:=False

appXL.ActiveWorkbook.SaveAs Left(strOpenFile,
Len(strOpenFile) - 4) &
"Simon.xls"
appXL.Quit
Set appXL = Nothing

End Sub
```

This macro starts by clicking a command button in the Access form.

Can you help me correct this problem?

A: Using ActiveWorkbook, and using Range and Selection (without an object reference) creates a new reference to the workbook file that keeps the instance of EXCEL running.

Try this:

```
Private Sub cmdImport_Click()

Dim appXL As New Excel.Application
Dim XLwb As Object
appXL.Visible = True
```

```
Dim strOpenFile As String
strOpenFile = appXL.GetOpenFilename("Excel Files
(*.xls), *.xls", , "Select
..xls file")

If strOpenFile = "False" Then
appXL.Quit
Exit Sub
End If

Set XLwb = appXL.Workbooks.Open(strOpenFile)

XLwb.Range("J:J,L:L,O:U,W:W,Z:AB,AD:AD").Select
XLwb.Selection.Replace What:=" ", Replacement:="",
LookAt:=xlPart, _
SearchOrder:=xlByRows, MatchCase:=False,
SearchFormat:=False,
ReplaceFormat:=False

XLwb.SaveAs Left(strOpenFile, Len(strOpenFile) - 4) &
"Simon.xls"
XLwb.Close
Set XLwb = Nothing
appXL.Quit
Set appXL = Nothing

End Sub
```

Question 21: Open Excel file - Forms Coding

I have an Excel document that is password protected for modifications; it pops a message box to the user asking for password or Read Only.

What I need to do is to open the Excel file from a command button, but the Excel message box to the user is behind the main form. I have to ALT+TAB to locate the Excel icon to get focus on Excel.

How can I open this document and force the Excel prompt to get focus?

A: Here is one way to open an Excel workbook via VBA:

```
Dim OpenExcel As Variant
Dim ExcelFile as String
ExcelFile = "C:\YourPath\YourFile.xls"
OpenExcel = Shell("Excel.exe " & ExcelFile , 0)
```

To accomodate a path and/or filename that has spaces, use this:

```
Dim OpenExcel As Variant
Dim ExcelFile as String
ExcelFile = "C:\Your Path\Your File.xls"
OpenExcel = Shell("Excel.exe " & """" & ExcelFile &
"""", 0)
```

It's the quadruple quotes that do it.

Question 22: Excel Shortcut Opens Visual Basic

When I double click any of my MS Excel icons/shortcuts, Visual Basic opens instead of excel. I'm currently using MS Office 2000 Professional, and I'm not sure what the problem is.

How do I sort this out?

A: A possible explanation to your problem is your Excel file association may be lost. You can try the following:

Start>Run "excel.exe /regserver"(no quotes and note the space before the / mark).

You may have to enter your full path to excel.exe. In that case surround with quotes as in:

"C:\mypath\to Excel\somewhere\excel.exe" /regserver

If this doesn't solve your problem, try to un-register first then go back to /regserver as above.

Start>Run "excel.exe /unregserver"(no quotes and note the space before the / mark).

If the above step still does not solve your problem, try this further.

Go to Start>Settings>Folder>Options>File Types. Scroll down to MS Excel Worksheet. If running Win98 OS Edit> select "Open" and Edit.

If using WinXP OS you would scroll down to .XLS then "Advanced">Open>Edit.

In Command line, the path should be similar to this if you want Book1 to open.

"C:\PROGRAM FILES\MICROSOFT
OFFICE\OFFICE\EXCEL.EXE" /e (delete the <sp>/e

You must have the double quotes.

Below have "use DDE" checked and this in the DDE message
box, [open("%1")].

Application should read "Excel"(no quotes).

Question 23 Copy - Special Paste - Transpose

I have a large listing of data that is downloaded from a data base
in a vertical format or has mulitple columns.

I there an easier way to copy and paste this data which will
always be a constant set of rows (over 300) and columns which
are approximately 10 columns?

I tried to download the data into (example) cells A1 through H1
(across) and A1 through A300 or A1:H300. The data set will be
every 12 (of the 300) rows will be for one group of items that
would have 12 weeks of data and 10 columns of varied
comparisons such as "Actual Hours", "Plan Hours", "SPLY
Hours", "Variance to Actual Hours", etc.

I like to drop this data set into Excel and copy each set of 12 rows
and data within the respective columns. I was unabe to complete
a copy - paste special - values - transpose. Excel did not allow me
to transpose such a large group of data; however, I was able to
copy and paste / special / transpose each group of 12
rows/columns.

How do I do this?

A: A Pivot Table can easily do what you want, but you need to
add a column that differentiates between the groups of 12.

For example, assuming your data is in A1:H300, and your
headers are in row 1, and your week 'number' is in column A,

then in column I in cell I2 put the following formula and copy down:-

`=COUNTIF($A$2:$A2,A2)`

This will then give you the values 1,1,1,.... 2,2,2,2..... 3,3,3,3 etc.

Label the column "Group" or something of your preference. Now just pivot, throw the Group number into the ROW fields, and drag the week number into the COLUMN fields.

You might have to reorder the week number slightly because your values are text and will not order the way you expect. Right click on wk 10 an choose order / move to end, then repeat for wk 11 and 12.

One by one, drag your numeric data into the DATA field.

Also, you don't need to fit 300 rows horizontally; that wouldn't be a useful representation of your data, at least not based on the example you gave us. By adding the helper column I described and laying the data out in that fashion,.

Question 24: Excel shared file conflicts

We have a shared Excel file that only allow 1 person at a time to do any editing while the rest of the people have to view as read only. We have to know who has the file opened and did any editing.

Is there a way for multiple users to edit on the single file at the same time?

A: A big consideration is which changes will be implemented. The reason only one person can edit at a time is so that changes are committed before other changes can be made. Imagine if two people were editing the same cell at the same time. Which edit would be the one to commit?

Sharepoint allows multiple users to edit the same file, but each will be given its version control. Sharepoint allows you to implement version control so that you can keep track of changes.

Question 25: Excel: Separate parts of name from one cell into separate cells

I have one cell with a filename. I need to separate it into three cells; one each for first, middle and last.

How do you accomplish this task?

A: You can do this with LEFT, MID and RIGHT. The start position, end position and length can be determined using FIND or SEARCH:

```
fname: =LEFT(A1,FIND(" ",A1)-1)
mi:    =MID(A1,FIND(" ",A1)+1,FIND(" ",A1,FIND("
",A1)+1)-FIND(" ",A1))
lname: =RIGHT(A1,FIND(" ",A1,FIND(" ",A1)))
```

Question 26: Show specific dates in Excel chart

I'm creating a graph in Excel. Because the data only shows certain dates, how do I customise the chart so it only shows the dates in the sheet and not every date between two periods?

For example, the source data contains events which occured Tuesday 1st, Wednesday 2nd and Friday 4th. There is no data for the other dates.

When I make the chart, it includes the dates which are not in the table (like Thursday 3rd, Saturday 6th).

The chart contains data over a 3 month period and I only got events recorded against 3 days of the week; each date shows up on the chart which makes it very long given the fact that over half of it is irrelevant.

I can't use AutoFilter because the data is only those dates when an event occured.

Can you give any solution for this?

A: Your x-axis can be EITHER a CATEGORY or TIME VALUE. You select this in Chart Options.

The difference is that CATEGORY plots each value as an isolated item without regard to it relative value, where TIME is relative. For example;

```
CAT:  1   3   6
TIM:  1  .  3  .  .  6
```

Question 27: Formula help: Use sheetName as a variable

I have a summary page that looks up various pieces of data in other pages (same workbook). I like to copy the formulas down instead of editing (or find/replace although that is an option).

For example:

```
sheetName    formula
sheet1       =if(sheet1!A1=sheet1!A2,"OK","ERR")
sheet2
```

If I copy the formula down to the next cell, I want sheet1 replaced by sheet2 (the value in the cell to the left).

How do I fix this?

A: You need to take a look at the INDIRECT function. Concatenate the sheet name and the cell reference.

Question 28: IF and OR statements

I like to use OR in an IF statement. The one I have right now is :

`=IF(A13="UNITED STATES ",A13,"")`

I tried to use:

`=IF((A13="UNITED STATES " OR A13="JAPAN"),A13,"")`

But I got an error. The search function is not working on this website.

Can you help me out?

A: Yes. Use this instead:

`=IF(OR(A13="UNITED STATES",A13="JAPAN"),A13,"")`

You may also use:

`=IF(OR(A13={"UNITED STATES","JAPAN"}),A13,"")`

Question 29: Excel macro to cut cell values in half

I am trying to create a macro that will divide by 2 the value of all the selected cells.

Is this possible?

I also tried to come up with a macro that will divide by 2 each individual selected cell but I can´t edit the cell but only write in it.

Can you give a solution if this is possible?

A: There is a non-VBA solution to this.

- In an empty cell, type in 2
- Copy that cell
- Select the range you want divided
- Right Click, select Paste Special then Divide
- Click OK

Once you know how to do something, you can always generate a macro by turning on your macro recorder (Tools > Macro > Record New Marco) and go through the steps.

Question 30: Search & replace a question mark

I want to replace a string in an excel column that has question marks but I don't want the "?" to be a wildcard.

My column has a lot of numbers like:

1235F??
abcdFAB
IEoac9oF99
acof??

I want to replace "F??" with "A??" and leave all the other F's alone.

Can you give any tips on how to do this?

A: You can try any of these two:

Click on the "Match Case"

Or:

Find: f~?
Replace: A?

Question 31: How to return code actively back to Access from Excel

From within Access (XP), I opened an Excel workbook and run a macro in that workbook. The last action the Excel macro does is to save and close that workbook. My problem is the VBA code in Access fails instead of running the next line of code in Access.

How do I get Access to continue running after the Excel macro has closed the workbook?

I want to keep Excel open for other uses later in the code so only the workbook is closed.

Both the Access DB and the Excel workbook are on the local C: drive and not being run over a network. Permissions are not an issue.

Access gives me the error code 440 Method 'Run' of object'_Application' failed.

Here is the sub:

```
CODE
Public Sub subOpenExcelWorkbookAndRunMacro()
On Error GoTo RangeNamed_ErrorHandling

Dim appExcel As Excel.Application
Dim strNameOfXlMacro As String

'   with Reference set to Excel Object Library

On Error Resume Next
'   Attempt to bind to an open instance of Excel
Set appExcel = GetObject(, "Excel.Application")

    If Err.Number <> 0 Then
        '   if Excel not open _
            then clear error
        Err.Clear
        '   and open Excel
        Set appExcel = CreateObject _
                ("Excel.Application")
```

```
    End If

'   restore normal error handling
On Error GoTo RangeNamed_ErrorHandling

'   open the workbook
appExcel.Workbooks.Open _
("C:\MyFolderName\MyExcelWorkbookName.xls")

'   set the Excel session to be visible
appExcel.Application.Visible = True

'   run the Excel macro
appExcel.Run ("NameOfMyExcelMacro")

'#########
'#  Excel marco runs and finishes
'#  by saving and closes workbook.
'#  Code does not get past here.
'#  error code: 440
'#  desc: method 'Run' of object'_Application failed
'#########

'   do more stuff
MsgBox "Excel is done." & vbCr & _
       "Now doing more stuff."

Exit Sub
RangeNamed_ErrorHandling:

MsgBox "Error handling actions and message goes
here." & vbCr & _
vbCr & _
"The error description is: " & vbCr & _
Err.Description & vbCr & _
vbCr & _
"The error type number is: " & vbCr & _
Err.Number _

End Sub
```

Can you give any idea on how to do this?

A: Try to make the Excel Macro just do the calulations; then have Access save and close the workbook.

You can try this:

CODE

```
'   run the Excel macro
appExcel.Run ("NameOfMyExcelMacro")

'   do more stuff
MsgBox "Excel is done." & vbCr & _
       "Now doing more stuff."

'   save and close the workbook
appExcel.ActiveWorkbook.Close (True)
```

Question 32: Change Servers

I have an Excel spreadsheet that imports data from SQL Server via the Import External Data query. I want to change the server, but can't find anything on how to do this.

Do you have any ideas on how to do this?

A: Yes, but it will take VBA codes to do what you want. You can do the following:

1) Turn on your macro recorder.

2) Edit the query. In the QBE grid, just Edit/Return data to Excel. Turn off the recorder.

3) Alt+F11 to toggle between the VB Editor and the active sheet.

4) In the VB Editor, observe your recorded code. You will see a Connection parameter with text that is assigned. This is where your server is specified. Change it accordingly.

As a matter of practice, I code almost all my MS Query queries this way. There's always a chance that a server will change. If others run the query, they often have servers mapped to different drives. You can assure that the server connection be drive-independent, via the connect string.

Question 33: Excel Text Formatting Formulas

I am cleaning a significant amount of address data in an Excel sheet. I have gotten to the P.O. Box portion of the list. This is formatted several different ways (i.e. PO Box, P.O. Box, P. O. Box, P O Box, etc.). The fastest way I can think to clean these is if I write a formula concatenating "P.O. Box" + the actual number. I can't seem to get a right formula to extract the box number since they vary in length.

Is there a way I can use some kind of a mid function to tell the formula to split the cell at the appropriate character number and use all data to the right of that point (without specifying the number of characters)?

A: If the "P. O. Box 2345" is in cell C2, then the formula is:

`=RIGHT(C2, LEN(C2)- FIND("x",C2))`

The formula gives you the box number and then you would concatenate it with whatever you prefer.

You can also use this:

`=MID(C2,FIND("x",C2)+1,255)`

Question 34: Calculated cell reference in a formula

I have this scenario:

1) A cell contains an integer, for example 6.
2) I want to put the following formula in another cell:

  `=sum(a1:a6)`

Where the 'a6' is constructed using the '6' from #1.

Is this possible, and what would the formula be?

A: Yes, it is possible. Here is one way:

  `=SUM(A1:INDEX(A:A,C1))`

C1 has the value of 6, or the calculation value.

Also, take a look at the OFFSET function.

`=Sum(OFFSET(A1,0,0,C1,1))`

C1 contains 6.

Question 35: Multiplying a column

If I have some values in column A that needs to be multiplied by 10, how do I do that?

How about if some cells are empty in the column and after multiplying by 10, I don't want the empty cells to be displayed?

A: For your first question, do the following:

Enter 10 in a blank cell. Under Edit menu, use Copy.

Highlight the cells in the column, then under Edit menu, choose Paste Special, then multiply.

For the second question, do the following:

Enter 10 in a blank cell. Under Edit menu, use Copy.

Highlight the cells in column, Press F5, click on Special, select Constants, then go to Edit menu, choose Paste Special, then Multiply.

The downside to this is that you lose the underlying data, albeit that may not matter. Personally, I prefer to keep the raw data and then have the multiplication factor out in another cell so that I can see what I am actually doing to that raw data.

In case that was of interest, it can be achieved by using a helper cell, for example, A1. In that cell put a value of 10. Now in any other blank cell, put in the formula =$A$1.

Now copy that cell with the formula, select all your records as previously described, and then do Edit / Paste Special / Multiply / Formulas.

You will now see that every cell of your data contains the original value but is now also multiplied by the value in cell A1, and any change to this value will be reflected in your data. Setting it back to 1 puts your data back as it was.

You can also now delete the helper cell that contained the =$A$1 bit.

Question 36: Excel 2003 protect formula form acidental type over

I am using Access to partially fill in a spreadsheet from an .XLT file. There are formulas in a few columns.

What can I do to prevent users from accidentally typing over the formulas of the spreadsheet?

Here is my code for reference.

```
CODE
    Dim oApp As Object
    Dim SheetName As String
    Set oApp = CreateObject("Excel.Application")

    'load document
    oApp.Workbooks.Add ("C:\AirMonitoring\Personnel
Air Sampling Log.xlt")

    ' save as new document
    SheetName =
"C:\AirMonitoring\Spreadsheets\PersonnelAirSamplingLo
g-" & Me.Project_Number & ".xls"
    oApp.ActiveWorkbook.SaveAs SheetName

    ' make Excel visible
    oApp.Visible = True

    ' fill in cells
    oApp.Application.Cells(2, 2).Value = Me.Facility
    ...
```

A: You need to do these steps:

1) Unlock all other cells that the user can change.

2) Protect the sheet.

Question 37: Excel/CSV Time Zone Change Formula

I have a CSV that I open in Excel 2007, containing a list of events with their start times and end times. However, the start time and end times are in Eastern Time and I'm in Central time. Before I can upload this list into Outlook, I need to change all these times to be minus 1 hour.

An example:

Event   Start   Finish
Meeting A 12:00:00 PM 1:00:00 PM
Meeting B 2:00:00 PM   2:30:00 PM
Meeting C 11:30:00 AM 12:30:00 PM

How do I start with this one?

A: An easy way will be to subtract 0.04166666 from the original value.

Another way is to use:

```
=A1-TIMEVALUE("1:00:00")    (for that matter,
TIMEVALUE("1:") will work, too)
=A1-TIME(1,,)
=A1-(1/24)    (1/24 of a day is 1 hour)
```

Question 38: Excel cell copying problem

I have a spreadsheet that I am trying to keep as dynamic as possible, so I can generate scripts from user entered data.

I have a column that I like to populate with the same formula all the way down:

Column 1
=C3
=C3
=C3

If I drag the top cell down, it populates as:

Column 1
=C3
=C4
=C5

How do I copy exactly what is in one cell all the way down?

A: To keep the exact same cell references when you copy, you have to make them absolute. You can use the F4 shortcut while clicked in the cell reference in the formula bar.

Question 39: Eliminating 'extra' rows when importing Excel files

When I import Excel files (for example, into a mapping software or other software that reads XLS files), sometimes more rows are imported than the contained actual data. If I open the offending workbook in Excel and press End-Home to find the end of the active range, the cell pointer jumps to a row several rows beyond the end of the actual data. Deleting the rows between the end of the data and the end of the active range does nothing. If I copy just the data to a new sheet and delete the old sheet, then the data imports correctly.

Is there an easier solution than creating a new sheet?

A: The used range resets only after you have saved the workbook.

Try this:

1) Do to the row just after your populated range.
2) Select the entire row.
3) Press [Ctrl]+[Shift]+[Down Arrow] to select all the way to the end of the sheet.
4) Right Click anywhere in the selected cells
5) Choose Delete
6) Save the file.

Now open the file again to see the changes.

Question 40: "average/if" statement

I tried to write an average/if statement that has a data which looks like:

30%
-55%
0%
83%
-33%

I like to write a statment that shows me the average IF the numbers are <0, and then a separate statement that shows average if >0.

How do I fix this?

A: You should never average averages. Consider the following example:

A) 10 out of 1000 = 1%

B) 20 out of 2000 = 1%

C) 9 out of 10 = 90%

The average of the averages is 31%.

The sum of 10, 20 and 9 is 39. The sum of 1000, 2000 and 10 is 3010. Dividing 39 by 3010 gives you 1.3%. 1% vs 31 % is a big difference.

A better process will be to work with the data where the percentages you quote came from in the first place. Using that raw data, sum the positives in one column and the correlating denominators in the second column, then divide those to come up with a correct percentage. Repeat for negatives.

Example formulas:

For positives:

```
=SUMIF(A1:A5,">0")/SUMPRODUCT((A1:A5>0)*(B1:B5))
```

For negatives:

```
=SUMIF(A1:A5,"<0")/SUMPRODUCT((A1:A5<0)*(B1:B5))
```

Question 41: Counting if two parameters are met

In Excel 2003, I tried to count the number of occurences where the date falls within a specified range as one parameter and where a cell contains a number which starts with any four digits as the second parameter (for example nnnn*).

I have produced the following first cut:

```
=SUM(IF(Consolid!$I$2:$I$14000,">1/2/07"),IF((LEFT(Co
nsolid!$A$2:$A$14000,4)="2520"),1,0))
```

The individual logic tests work fine; it is when I assemble them that I run into problems.

How do I correct this problem?

A: Try this:

```
=SumProduct((LEFT(Consolid!$A$2:$A$14000,4) = "2520")
* (Consolid!$I$2:$I$14000 > DateValue("01/02/2007")))
```

Question 42: Trim In Place for Excel

I like to know how to do a Trim in place for Excel, instead of having to do it from a reference cell/column. I don't want the cell content to look like =TRIM(A1).

I tried this:

```
Copy > paste special > values afterwards
```

Is there another way of doing this without having to send a big-sized file?

A: Try the following macro. It deletes leading and trailing spaces from values but not formulae, in the selection. Non-breaking space characters (CHR (160)) are also processed, by changing them first to normal spaces. The macro also reduces internal spaces to a single space. Use Trim(Cell.Value) instead of Application.Trim(Cell.Value) to retain the original internal spacing.

Question 43: Hide FALSE

I like to hide cells where the formula displays "FALSE". Turning the text white would be suffcient but I can't get it to work with conditional formatting.

I tried using ISERROR but FALSE isn't really an error so that didn't help. I think there is a way to make a formula read FALSE as text but I don't know how to do that. I just want to supress FALSE from displaying.

The actual formula I'm using is:

```
=IF(D8>0,IF($E$4>0,(D8-AB8)/$E$4,ABS(AH8)))
```

```
D8 = quota
$E$4 = # days left in the month
AB8= mtd commissions
AH*= +/- quota
```

What it's saying is, if you have a quota and there are still days left in the month, subtract your current commissions from your quota and divide that by the # of days left in the month to get your target for today. On the last day of the month the # of days left = 0 so instead of dividing by 0, I used the IF statement to just give me the current total of whatever they are ahead or behind. The FALSE is resulting from people who have no quota assigned to them.

Can you suggest any solution to this?

A: Try this.

Conditional format:

[cell value] is [equal to] False

Or, in your formula,

```
=IF(D8>0,IF($E$4>0,(D8-AB8)/$E$4,ABS(AH8)),"")
```

Question 44: Sending data between worksheets

I have a spreadsheet with usually around 100 leads a day in it. I have 20 sales people I distribute the leads to every morning.

Is there a way to add 20 worksheets to my spreadsheet and distribute the leads evenly among the sales staff? Each new worksheet would represent a sales person.

It is best if I can distribute them like this:

Lead 1 to Ralph
Lead 2 to Shannon
Lead 3 to Vicky
Etc...
Lead 21 to Ralph
Lead 22 to Shannon...

I don't want the first 10 leads going to the first sales person's worksheet the next 10 to the next worksheet and so on.

My lead spreadsheet has 4 columns and 100 rows of data; the worksheet with the leads is named "Leads" and the columns are:

Date	FirstName	LastName	State
3/27	John	Johnson	PA
3/27	Jim	Bob	TN
3/27	Kathy	Kipler	MA
3/27	Anthony	Sky	FL

I want all the data from Leads worksheet row1 to go to salesperson1 on sheet1 (their worksheet), row2 goes to salesperson2 on sheet2, etc. Once I get through my 20 salespeople, who will each have 1 lead now, I want row21 (or lead 21) to go to salesperson1 on worksheet1 row2 and continue parsing the data until all the leads are assigned to a salesperson.

I want to be able to import new leads into this workbook and start the process over again everyday.

Is this possible? Can you help me with this?

A: Yes, try the following:

1) On a separate sheet, make a list of salespersons, and give it a range name Sales_Persons.

2) On a separate sheet, have your leads starting in A2, Heading in A1.

3) In E2:

```
=INDEX(Sales_Persons,MOD(ROW()-
2,COUNTA(Sales_Persons))+1,1)
```

And copy down through your list.

4) Turn on AutoFilter

Or:

4) Create a PivotTable on 20 sheets with the Sales Person in the Page Field.

5) Filter on each Sales Person

Question 45: Show minutes from a time calulation

I have two time entries named Start and End, with values 8:00 and 16:00 respectively. I need to calculate how many minutes between this two, which is 480 minutes or 8 hours. I am having difficulty in formatting the cell to show this.

My formula is =C9-C4 Where C9 is the end time, C4 the start time. Right now it shows 8:00, but I need it shown in minutes which have the value 480.

Can you help me with this?

A: You can see what you need covered in detail in the Excel Help (see Difference between two times).

Excel stores dates as whole numbers and time as a fraction of a day. To quote the Help:

"Present the result in a total based on one time unit (120 minutes). To do this task, use the INT function, or HOUR, MINUTE, and SECOND functions.

To copy an example:

Formula Description (Result)
=INT((B2-A2)*24) Total hours between two times (28)
=(B2-A2)*1440 Total minutes between two times (1735)
=(B2-A2)*86400 Total seconds between two times (104100)
=HOUR(B2-A2) Hours between two times, when the difference does not exceed 24. (4)
=MINUTE(B2-A2) Minutes between two times, when the difference does not exceed 60. (55)
=SECOND(B2-A2) Seconds between two times, when the difference does not exceed 60. (0)"

Question 46: Month Name from single number

I have a user who has a spreadsheet with exported data. The month is listed as a single number, 1 through 12. The user wants to show these numbers on another sheet by the month's name.

For example: 1 = Jan, 2 = Feb, etc.

Do you know how to do this?

A: Try using this formula:

`=DATE(2007,Sheet1!A1,1)`

And use custom format.

Question 47: Excel line total

I'm working on a sheet that I need a cell to total in. I want this cell to add up until it reaches 25,000. When it reaches 25,000, it will hold on this number.

For example, cell G18 is a total of two cells and can range from 0 to unlimited and cell H18 is set at 75%. I need a cell to multiply the G18 x H18 and total from 0 to 25,000 but cap at 25,000. I need the capped cell to start a new string of formulas.

How I can accomplish this?

A: Try using:

`=min(G18*H18,25000)`

Question 48: Count based on 2 criteria

I have a table like this:

Server Brand Type

ABC   Sun   Server
BCD   Sun   Tape Drive
EFG   Dell Server
JKL   Sun   Server

Result 2

If the row matches to "Sun" and "Server", I like to count it and the result should be 2. I tried function "match" or "if" but it's not successful.

How do I make this work?

A: Yes, try using this:

`=SUMPRODUCT(--(B1:B10="Sun"),--(C1:C10="Server"))`

Question 49: Can not see sheet 2

I have an Excel file. I can see sheet1, but not sheet2, and I know that it is there.

How will I be able to see sheet2?

A: Try the following:

[Ctrl]+[Page Up] and [Ctrl]+[Page Down]; these will scroll through non-hidden worksheets.

If you still can't find the sheet, it may be hidden. Go to Format > Sheet > Unhide to see if Sheet2 was hidden.

Question 50: Excel "If Statement" Based on Format

Is there a way to say "IF A1 is Bold THEN 'It's Bold' ELSE 'it's Not Bold'".

I think the Excel Formula would look something like:

```
=IF(A1.font = "BOLD", "It's Bold", "It's Not
Bold")It's the ".font = "BOLD"
```

Is this correct or did I miss something?

A: There is no way to get a format with native spreadsheet code.

Insert this function in a module, preferably in your Personal.xls.

```
CODE
Function IsBold(rng As Range)
    If rng.Font.Bold Then
        IsBold = True
    Else
        IsBold = False
    End If
End Function
```

You can use like any other IS Function.

Question 51: EXCEL - count per timeframe, without each one listed

I have a spreadsheet that has several columns of data, one being a "start date" and another an "end date". I want to be able to take look at this data and say how many records were eligible for a specific month, without having to list each month. Below is a small sample:

```
12345  Smith   1/1/2006   12/31/2006
23456  Jones   1/1/2006   11/30/2006
34567  Taylor  3/1/2006   11/30/2006
```

Is there some kind of a formula I can use to count how many were eligible in January 2006 (2), or December 2006 (1), or February 2006 (2), or May 2006 (3), etc.?

A: You can use this:

```
=sumproduct(--
(Start_Date<=MyDate)*(End_Date>=MyDate))
```

```
Where Start_Date & End_Date are named ranges and
MyDate (also a named range for one cell) has a real
date.
```

Question 52: Excel copy / paste help

No amount of analysing recorded macros has helped me to figure out how to do what I need.

I have sheet names in row 2. Let's say my active cell is row 5 column 7. I want to copy cells a5:e5 from the sheet name stored in column 7 rows 2 to sheet display row 1 column 1.

Can you point me in the right direction?

A: Try this:

CODE

```
ActiveSheet.Range(Cells(ActiveCell.row, "A"),
Cells(ActiveCell.row, "E")).Copy Sheets(Cells(2,
ActiveCell.Column).value).Cells(1,1)
```

Question 53: Hidden Characters Excel 2003

I have an Excel spreadsheet that takes you way out beyond the last cell with data in it when you press control+end. I know that there are hidden characters (crlf?) in these cells, but I was unable to delete them. Highlighting and pressing delete doesn't work and selecting the rows and removing them doesn't work either.

Do you know how to remove the unwanted characters?

A: Try this:

After deleting any unwanted characters, highlight the whole spreadsheet; go to Format, then Row, and then Autofit.

Question 54: Excel: Text with * in formulas

I am working with a simple IF/OR formula in Excel wherein I want to return one of several predetermined values based on the content in the reference cell. The data in the cell is text and I tried to use a wildcard to match the criteria so that if just part of the text string is in the cell, it will be a match.

Here is the code:

```
CODE
=IF(OR(OR(F3="text1"),OR(F3="text2")),LOOKUP(F3,{"tex
t1","text2"},{"35-40","28-32"}),"30-35")
```

This works if the value is matched exactly; but if I surround the value with wildcards like this "*text1*" it only matches the value *text1*. This is easy in Access where the following statement will return any permutation of text1.

```
CODE
Like "*" &[text1] & "*"
```

How is this done in Excel?

A: Use the FIND function and ISNA to determine not found.

Note: Find is case-sensitive while Search is not.

Example:

```
=if(isnumber(search("text1", F3)), "35-40",
if(isnumber(search("text2", F3)), "28-32", "30-35"))
```

87

Question 55: Manipulate Pivot Table Criteria

Is there a way to reference the data in a pivot table field in order to manipulate the data?

For example, I have a month field and I want to be able to choose a month "month 10" and have the month fields on my Pivot table show Month <=10, so 1-10, but "click off" months 11 and 12.

A: The first thing I will do is to add another field to your source data that fed from the selections chosen on the other sheet.

Assume you already have a field in your data called Month, and that contains values such as 1-12. You can now have another field that looks at that value and then using something like COUNTIF, look at the selected options on another sheet and determine whether or not that record will fall within the selection criteria. This will give you a load of TRUE/FALSES in that field.

Now drag it into the page fields, filter on TRUE, and then have the code refresh the Pivot table every time the selection criteria are changed.

You can use it all the time, especially for date parameters, which makes it l easy to constrain your data to within two dates. For example, using an existing date field and a simple >= and a <= comparison against two specific dates elsewhere in the file.

Also use it to put into groupings the data where it does not exist, using the same principle.

Question 56: Combine text and date display in word wrapped cell

I want to display "Posted on Mar 14" as a column label. The date portion is to be grabbed from another cell. I also want the label to be word wrapped so it doesn't take up much space.

I have tried using:

```
=Concatenate("Posted on ", A1)
```

And it wraps fine but I can't make the date to display in date format; it only shows "Posted on 39155" no matter how I try to configure the formatting.

I have tried custom formatting the cell and inserting the test before the value but the results won't wrap.

Can you give suggestions concerning this?

A: You need the date to be formatted to display correctly. Look at the Text function; I am not sure that I understand the value of the concatenate function. This will work just as well:

```
="posted on "&TEXT(A1,"DD MMM YY")
```

Also, to force wrapping after ="posted on", you could code the formula as:

```
="posted on"&CHAR(10)&TEXT(A1,"DD MMM YY")
```

Question 57: Refer to named cell

How can I get Excel to recognize that I want to refer to a defined name and not just the actual words?

Example:

A1	B1	C1
Chill	=A1&C1	Out

A200 is a cell named ChillOut and its contents are blabla. I want cell B1 to display blabla not the word chillout. I know it will work if I just typed =chillout in cell B1 but I want it calculated based on what is in another cell.

Can you help me with this?

A: Try this:

A1	B1	C1
Chill	=indirect(A1&C1)	Out

Question 58: Find/Replace Question

I have a column of numbers ranging from 1 to 15. Each number indicates a location name. I like to conduct a find/replace on each of these numbers and change it to the location name, for example, the number "1" becomes "London".

When I tried to find the number "1", it replaces every "1" in the column, replacing "11" with "LondonLondon".

Do you know the correct syntax for doing this?

A: You need to change the 2 digit numbers first.

Question 59: Zoom in on a Chart in Excel

I am using Excel 2003 and Window XP. I have a chart in an Excel file that was created by someone else. I like to zoom in on the chart to see some of the data in order to add an arrow pointing to a specific portion of the chart (a line chart). When I tried to zoom, this option is grayed out. View menu Zoom is also grayed out.

The chart is not on the same page as the data. It appears to be linked via formula to a different tab in the file. Since I can't see any empty cells, I tried clicking to deselect the chart, but zoom is still unavailable.

Can you help me figure this out?

A: If it's on a different worksheet, it may be sized with window. Select View > Sized with window and try turning it off (if it is selected).

In cases where you can't get the sizing to turn off, you may need to recreate the chart. If you do recreate, you need to go to options > chart tab and make sure that the "chart sized with window frame" checkbox is turned off.

Question 60: Function to add leading zeroes to make a 4 digit number

I have an Excel spreadsheet with a long list of numbers on it (over 1500). Some of the numbers are less than four digits (like 23) and I need them to all be converted to four digit numbers with leading zeroes (like 0023).

I have already converted that column to text so it will display the leading zeroes. Rather than search through the list and manually edit the numbers to add the leading zeroes, I wrote a function to do this; the function is called "Modify_Barcodes", but it does not work.

Here is the code:

```
Public Function Modify_Barcodes(Orig_Numb As
String)
'Created 3/7/07 by Scott Wasmer
'This function will take a number of less than
four digits
'and add leading zeroes to it so as to make it
have four digits.
'eg - 23 would modify to 0023

    'Declare some variables
    Dim intOrig_String As Integer
    Dim intZeros_2_Add As Integer


    'Detemine the number of leading zeroes to
add
    intOrig_String = Len(Orig_Numb)
    intZeros_2_Add = 4 - intOrig_String

    'Now concantanate the string with the
zeroes.
        Select Case intZeros_2_Add

        Case 0
            Orig_Numb = Orig_Numb
        Case 1
            Orig_Numb = "0" & Orig_Numb
        Case 2
            Orig_Numb = "00" & Orig_Numb
        Case 3
            Orig_Numb = "000" & Orig_Numb
        Case Else
        'Put some error routine here

    End Select

End Function
```

I tried it both as passing the number in as a string and an integer; also tried schemes of getting the value or the string, etc. I always get the same result.

For example, if in cell A23 there is the number 23 and then in cell E23 I type =Modify_Barcodes(A23) the only thing I get in E23 is 0.

When I put breakpoint in the code, all the variables have the correct values. After the line:

Case 2
```
        Orig_Numb = "00" & Orig_Numb
```

I put in a Debug.Print Orig_Numb statement, and then in the immediate window I got the result of 00 23. I was not sure of why there is a space either. But in the cell on the worksheet, all I get is 0.

Can you correct me if there is an error in my method?

A: There's a difference between DISPLAYING leading zeros for numbers and CONVERTING numbers to TEXT with leading zeros.

For displaying, select the range:

Cells/Format - Number Tab - Custom in the TYPE box 0000

For converting, you cannot use a function to change the value in the cell. You can return a value to another cell, and:

```
=TEXT(A1,"0000")
```

That is if your number is in A1.

93

Question 61: Create a conditional statement prior to closing a program

I have created a spreadsheet where the user is required complete entries/inputs into many different cells. The issue I have is that sometimes the user may omit entering data that is not always required from other users.

Is there a way to alert the user about that missed input of data at the time the user clicks the save button?

I like the system to create a test of data entered into various cells and if for example, Cell A1 has data then cell A2 should also have data entered by the user; presently, they may forget to input data into this cell A2.

Can this be done without using VBA?

A: This solution will not stop the user saving while the entries are incomplete but it will alert them and this does not need VBA.

Simple Example: There must be an entry in B2 if there is an entry in A2.

Cell A1 contains your error message. Use freeze panes to make sure the cell is always visible. Set the font coluor to white so that the error text cannot be seen.

```
Format, Conditional Format
Formula is: =AND(A2,NOT(B2))
```

Set the format if the above condition has been met to Font Colour Red.

Extend it to test many conditions in a different worksheet. Use formulae in cells A1 to A10 to test for the errors. For ease, give these cells a rangename of "MyTest". Set each of these formulae so the answer is 0 if there is no error or 1 if there is an error.

On the original worksheet, cell A1, change the formula for the conditional format to:

```
=sum(MyTest)>0
```

You can further develop it. Make Cell A1 a hyperlink to your list of errors (with useful explanations in column B. Set the text for the hyperlink to "Data entry incomplete - click here for details". Again make this white until the conditional format kicks in.

The trouble with this approach is that the error message is there all the time a record is part entered, so the user may just grow to ignore it.

Also check out Data, Validation.

Question 62: Ordering of year / month in a pivot table

I have a spreadsheet containing details of calls we have received. I need to show calls per week and month.

The date of the call is in A2. I used =YEAR(A2) and =MONTH(A2) to get the year and the month from the date, then put them together using =(C2)&" "&(D2).

This data then goes into a pivot table. However, the pivot table does not display the months in the correct order because they are formatted "2007 2" rather than "2007 02".

Can you tell me how to format the month like "02"?

A: You can use this:

```
=C2 & " " & rept("0",2-len(D2)) & D2
```

The "Rept" function repeats a text string for a specified number of occurences. This is calculated by using the length of the data in D2 and subtracting that from the maximum length of 2. If there are already 2 digits, there will be no repeating zeroes. If there is 1 digit, it will put a 0 in front of the value in D2

Also, if A1 is a DATE, try:

```
=TEXT(A1, "yyyy mm")
```

Try bringing the DATE into the PT, then use Group & Outline on the Date field, selecting Month & Year.

Question 63: Charting when data is above defined percentage

I have some data that was sampled every 5 seconds. The data is temperature.

How can I calculate the percentage of time when the temperature was above a certain point?

The data is from a data logger on a vehicle measuring exhaust temperature.

I also need to chart the information with a simple xy chart, including some way of noting in the chart the 40% mark.

Can you help me do this?

A: You need to find the count of all values.

Then if 70 degrees is your temperature limit, you can find the number of times it was over by:

```
=COUNTIF(C1:C200, ">70")
```

Where C1:C200 contains your temperature values. You can include this in your formula to count your percent.

```
=COUNTIF(C1:C200, ">70")/count(C1:C200)
```

If you want to chart it, just add a series with two points that define a straight horizontal line at 40%.

Question 64: Calculate Number of Digits

I work in a screen printing business and we print numbered bibs for sports events.

I created a spreadsheet for the number ranges required and then apply the following functions to calculate how many individual digits are required to be printed:

`left(), mid(), right(), countif()`

I wanted to setup a spreadsheet for my boss where he can simply enter the number in column A and then the calculation will automatically happen. For example:

Bib number range of 100 - 170 and a number range of 200 - 2500. From these ranges, I need to know how many 0's, how many 1's, how many 2's, etc.

The len() function only returns the length of the number.

Can you give me any suggestions on how to deal with this?

A: This should work for your situation:

```
=SUM(LEN(A1:A1000) - LEN(SUBSTITUTE(A1:A1000, B1,
"")))
```

Enter this as an array formula (use [Ctrl]+[Shift]+[Enter] instead of just enter). You will have to enter whatever number you want to be counted into cell B1.

Another way, which only requires you to have the first & last numbers in A1 & A2 respectively and the test digit in B1 is:

```
=SUM(LEN(ROW(INDIRECT($A1&":"&$A2)))-
LEN(SUBSTITUTE(ROW(INDIRECT($A1&":"&$A2)),B1,)))
```

Enter this as an array formula. If you have your digits 0-9 in
B1:K1, copying the formula across will give the quantities
required for all 10 digits.

Note that if dealing with an Array Formula, you have to use
[Ctrl]+[Shift]+[Enter] after you edit each time. You can use 10
different array formulas so you don't have to edit any of them.

Question 65: Conditional Sums Using Multiple Criteria Error

I tried to create a formula that sums the Revenue Column (Range Named "Revenue"); the Named Ranges Client="CR" AND Campaign="PCR". I have tried:

```
{=SUM((Client="CR")*(Campaign="PCR")*Revenue)}
```

I got the error "#NUM!"

I tried not to use an array and the result is not even close.

Will it make a difference if my named ranges are on a different sheet from where I am trying to put the formula?

A: You need to have precise definitions of your names. For example, if they are in entire columns, make them shorter by one row like $A$1:$A$65535 instead of $A:$A.

Question 66: formula does not show results

I am using MS Excel 2003. I have a simple formula that references the cell to its left.

Cell E2 has CD8003-22 in it. In cell F2 I have the formula =MID(E2,3,7). I don't see any results in F2, just the formula.

If I use the function wizard for cell F2, it displays the proper results in its dialog box.

What am I doing wrong? Is there a setting I need to check?

A: You need to go to Tools menu, then options, and then under View tab uncheck formulas.

A shortcut for these is CTRL+`.

Question 67: Splitting postcodes in Excel

I got a list of postcodes with the format 'xxx xxx'. I need to lose the last 2 digits in the postcode leaving me with 'xxx x'.

For example, I have the postcode 'PO2 4FR', but I only want the cell to contain 'PO2 4'.

Can you give a suggestion on how to accomplish this?

A: You need to take a look at Data/Text to columns.

Question 68: Macro to delete text

We currently export a report into Word from an external application. The report contains up to 200 .png check images; it also contained a lot of text that we have to look at and manually delete. All we want is the images of the checks.

Is there a Macro we can set-up in either Word or Excel that will delete all text and only leave the images on import or one that we can run once data is imported?

A: You can use this code in Excel.

CODE

```
Sub ClearText()
  dim ws as worksheet
  for each ws in worksheets
    ws.Cells.ClearContents
  next
End sub
```

Question 69: Data on the front side of checks

I received a report wherein the data is represented by images of checks, both the frontside and backside. The front and back images are in an alternating fashion (as in the front are odd and the back even). I only need the data represented by all the frontside of the checks.

Is there a code I can use to delete every other image or all the even or backside from the spreadsheet?

A: You can use this:

CODE:

```
sub DeleteEvenIndexShapes()
'odd index - front of check
'even index - back of check
  dim i as integer, ws as worksheets
  for each ws in worksheets
    for i = ws.shapes.count to 2 step -2
      ws.shapes(i).delete
    next
  next
end sub
```

Question 70: Tracking RDO's

I am trying to set up an Excel sheet for tracking employees "RDO's" (Reg. Days Off) but I am having this trouble. When A1 contains the date for the first of the month, G1 – AK1 equal the DayName and G2 – AK2 equal the Day number, 'AND', if, E4 contains "JS" (Sat/Sun), OR "SM" (Sun/Mon), OR "MT" (Mon/Tue), etc, the corresponding cell below the Day number will then auto fill "RDO" (Regular Day Off).

I tried using:

```
"=IF(AND(G1="Sun",E4="JS",OR(E4="SM","RDO",IF(AND(G1=
"Mon",E4="SM",OR(E4="MT","RDO",     . . .
etc.,etc.,etc.   . . .,"")))))))".
```

I either wind up with "########" in G1 or I get the "RDO", but for the whole week and not just the actual RDO day. When I change the date in A1 to the next month it all goes haywire.

Can you help me with this?

A: For an application like this to work seamlessly for any month, the VALUES in G1:AK1 must be dates; the first date referenced to A1 and each data after that a formula, adding one to the previous date. Format these cells to display DAY of the date.

G2:AK2 references the row 1 value and is formatted ddd to display three character day of date.

You need to build a table that decodes the days; the data range name is RDO_TABLE.

RDO	FR	TH
JS	0	1
SM	1	2
MT	2	3
TW	3	4
WT	4	5
TF	5	0
FS	6	1

Here is the RDO formula:

```
=IF(OR(VLOOKUP($E4,RDO_TABLE,2)=MOD(G$2,7),VLOOKUP($E
4,RDO_TABLE,3)=MOD(G$2,7)),"RDO","")
```

The table can be on any sheet. Typically, I place lookup tables on a separate sheet designated for that purpose.

1) Select the DATA range in the lookup table (exclude the headings).

2) In the Name box enter RDO_TABLE and hit ENTER.

The Name box is to the left of the Formula Bar. If your Formula Bar is not visible, go to Tools/Options - View tab - check Show Formula bar.

Check HELP on the VLOOKUP function in order to understand what's happening.

Question 71: Skipping Empty Cells When Plotting

I know I can go to chart options and select to "skip empty cells" when plotting a graph. The problem is, the way I have programmed my spreadsheet, the cells aren't technically empty.

I am averaging groups of cells to create my time series. When there is missing data for a certain time period, the equation is programmed to return a blank to avoid a DIV/0 error, like:

`=IF(ISNUMBER(AVERAGE(A3:A50)),AVERAGE(A3:A50),"")`

But if a period returns a blank value, instead of treating this as a true empty cell and skipping the point on my graph, Excel treats it as a zero.

Is there anyway around this? How can I force Excel to treat this as a true empty cell?

A: Instead of a formula, you must run a VBA procedure to populate your data.

Try using:

`=IF(ISNUMBER(AVERAGE(A3:A50)),AVERAGE(A3:A50),NA())`

Question 72: Excel 'Security Warning box'

I have my Excel security set to medium; it is necessary since there is important data on the system. But it always gives a warning for our own documents, stuff that holds a macro but is perfectly safe.

I did a research and found that I should be able to define our own documents as 'trusted source' using the 'Security Warning box'.

The problem is I can't find a 'Security Warning box'. Using Tools > Macro > Security, it has a tab called 'Trusted Sources', with nothing in it.

Can you guide me on how to do this?

A: Depending on your Excel version, this can be a general guide.

Go to Start, Programs, Microsoft Office, Microsoft Office Tools, and Digital Certificate for VBA Project. Create your signature.

Open your file with Macros, go to Visual Basic Editor, and highlight your project [for example, VBAProject(Book1.xls)]

Go to Tools, Digital Signature. Browse and find your signature.

Save & close file, close the application then start again, and Open the file.

At the Enable Macros prompt, check "Always trust macros from this publisher".

Question 73: capture find results

If I do a "find" across multiple worksheets, can I capture the information found and paste it in an unused column without VBA?

For example:
    Find "Africa" on all worksheets
    found "Africa" on sheet1
    found "Africa" on sheet4
    found "Africa" on sheet5

Paste in unused column.
A1   B1
Africa sheet1
Africa sheet4
Africa sheet5

A: Certainly. You just stop on each sheet and do a manual copy and paste, then enter the appropriate sheet name against each entry.

However, it cannot be automated without VBA.

Question 74: Finding Monday's date

What will the formula look like for finding Monday's date when it's not Monday?

For example, if the day were Thursday, January 18th 2007, the answer would be 1/15/2007.

Can you help me by also explaining the formula?

A: You can try:

`=A1-MOD(A1-2,7)`

The MOD function returns the remainder after divising one number by another. Thus, 13 MOD 10 (or MOD(13,10) in Excel parlance) is 3. If the number divides exactly, the remainder is 0.

All date values in Excel are just numbers, which when divided by 7 leave a remainder (0=Saturday to 6=Friday). Thus MOD(Date,7) returns the day of the week, with 0 being Saturday. If I deduct the raw MOD value from today's date, I'll get the most recent Saturday.

What I wanted to do in this case, was to find the most recent Monday. So, I needed to make Monday return 0 from the MOD function. Since the MOD value for Monday is 2, MOD(Date-2,7) returns 0 for Monday.

It's then a simple matter to deduct the MOD result from the date to return the most recent Monday.

Question 75: IF formula

I linked cells from one worksheet to another. I have found that if the "linked" cell does not contain anything, it returns a value of 0.

Is there a way to link cells so that the cell just remains blank?

A: Here are two ways to do what you want.

1) Go to Tools menu, then Options, then View, and then uncheck Zero values

Or:

2) In the Destination cell(s):
=IF(ISBLANK(SourceCell),"",SourceCell)

Question 76: Create Date from 3 Fields

I have 3 columns named, Day, Month and Year. I want to combine the 3 columns into one, and then import the spreadsheet into Access. The problem is that Access won't recognize the combined Date column as a date, but sees it as text.

What format should the Day, Month and Year columns be in so that when they are combined, the result is a date? I tried formating them as text, then using the formular A1&"/"&B1&"/C1, I then format the resulting column as a date, but Access still sees it as text.

A: Try this:

`=Date(Year,month,Day)`

so in your case it might be:

`=Date(C2,B2,A2)`

Question 77: Adding Column C & Selecting an array for a quartile formula

I'm currently working on a spreadsheet where I need to calculate a quartile based on data in one of the columns. However the data is categorised by a variable in a preceeding column. Here's an example:

Column A	Column B
Type 1	1.4
Type 1	2.8
Type 1	3.4
Type 1	1.2.....(for hundreds of rows, then...)
Type 2	3.6
Type 2	2.1
Type 2	2.0....etc...

I wish to include a column "C" which returns the top quartile for data items in each range defined by column A. For example, the top quartile for all of "type 1" data, to be shown in column C (so in effect, the same quartile value will be displayed next to all type 1 data items).

The spreadsheet is massive, with lots of different data types, so I would like to define the quartiles based on the ranges in column A through a formula that can be copied and pasted throughout the sheet.

In essence I would like to return the quartile in column C, and I know that this would be a duplicated value for the data items of any particular category.

I would just like to be able to extend the formula throughout the rest of the rows in column C, but the quartile calculated on arrays based on the categorics defined in column A.

So the structure would look like this:

Column A	Column B	Column C
Type 1	1.4	Quart all B values relating to type 1
Type 1	2.8	Quart all B values relating to type 1

Type 1	3.4 Quart all B values relating to type 1
Type 1	1.2 Quart all B values relating to type 1
Type 2	1.3 Quart all B values relating to type 2
Type 2	2.1 Quart all B values relating to type 2
Type 2	2.0 Quart all B values relating to type 2

etc...

I thought I could do a quartile with the "sumif" formula embedded in it like so:

```
=quartile(sumif(A$1:A$5000,A1,B$1:B$5000),1)
```

But obviously utilising a sum doesn't return the true quartile. In essence I need the formula to select the range of data items related to each type defined in column A.

A: You can start by naming the Ranges:

TYP VAL

Ranges begin in row 2.

```
=QUARTILE(OFFSET(A1,MATCH(A2,TYP,0),1,COUNTIF(TYP,A2)
,1),1)
```

This would save you about 2 hours of manually selecting ranges.

Question 78: Extract email address to another cell

I'm not even sure if there is a way to do this, but I'll ask. I have cells which show a users name along with their email address. They look like this:

john smith (jsmith@whatever.com)

I need to extract just the email address to another cell.

Is this possible? I don't want to have to go through each cell manually.

A: For data in A1:

`=MID(A1,FIND("(",A1)+1,LEN(A1)-FIND("(",A1)-1)`

`[MS MVP - Word]`

Question 79: Reverse data

I have data from 2007 to 1980.

Is it possible to chart the data from 1980 to 2007 (reverse the axis or something similar)?

A: The dates should default to low-to-high. If you want this reversed, then:

-Right click on the X axis.
-Select Format Axis.
-Go to the Scale tab.
-Check the box beside Dates in reverse order.

If your data doesn't default to low-to-high, you probably don't have the date column (in the source data) actually stored as numbers, but rather text. If this seems to be the case then you need to convert your text to numbers.

Or try a simpler method of doing a simple "reverse" in the Help for Excel.

Another alternative is to determine if your category falls under the axis, all you have to do is SORT the source data in a different order.

If the axis is a date-time axis, then you can select the axis, Format Seleted Axis - Scale tab and check - dates in reverse order.

Question 80: Resizing Document in Excel

Over a period of a couple of days, I will use the same file among several systems with different monitor screen sizes. Similar to other keyboard shortcuts (e.g. copy=ctrl key+c), is there a keyboard command for resizing the worksheet to the Excel window instead of dragging the edges or using maximize option (in upper right corner of Excel screen)?

A: Try using Alt - (Alt and hypen at the same time) followed by X. This should work.

Question 81: Automatically change DATE entry

I have a column of dates and would like the fomatting changed (bold, colour, etc) automatically if the date is over 3 years.

Any ideas how to do this?

A: Look at conditional formatting (menu command Format/Conditional Formatting), and choose Formula Is, with a condition formula of:

```
CODE
=A2<DATE(YEAR(TODAY())-3,MONTH(TODAY()),DAY(TODAY()))
changing A2 to whatever is suitable for you. Then
choose your formats.
```

Question 82: Totals on column chart

I have a column chart. Each rectangle represents represents several categories. I would like to show the total for each rectangle.

Example:

Year	cat.1	cat.2	total
1990	2	3	5
1991	6	3	9

If I draw a column chart of cat.1 and cat.2 per year, I would like to show the totals on top of the bar (5 and 9).

How can I do this?

A: This requires a little bit of imagination. Plot all your values including the totals in the chart.

Select the totals series, right click and change the Chart Type to a Line chart. Right click on the line chart, choose Format Data Series. On the Patterns tab, choose none for lines and for markers, so it's invisible; on the Data Labels tab, choose Show Values. Press OK.

Right click on the data labels, choose Format Data Labels and on the Alignment tab choose above for the option.

Question 83: Looking for a Different Chart

I am searching from a chart in Excel or Power Point that appears like a meter (the shape of a half moon) or like a meter in your car, that will allow for a range of numbers to be displaced (0 thru 100) within the "meter/ half moon shape" and will allow me to set a line (needle) that will show a score.

Any ideas or can someone lead me to a web site with additional charts in Excel or Power Point?

Note: I was able to draw such a chart / meter in Excel using "arrows or the format line options", but was unable to paste this drawing into this message. Can someone tell me why I am "unable" to paste drawings, like I am able to paste words?

I am sure there is some type of program that will allow a "meter" type chart.

Is there such a chart? If not, how can I do this?

A: I think you'll need to use VBA to insert and rotate autoshapes.

Just for kicks, as a starting point, I've got the following that draws a gauge and rotates the needle:

```
CODE
Public Function needle(gage As String, dial As
Single)
ActiveSheet.Shapes(gage).Rotation = dial
End Function

Public Function DrawGauge(onsheet, gaugename As
String, centx, centy, diameter As Integer)
radius = diameter / 2

DialLeft = centx - radius
DialTop = centy - radius
DialWidth = diameter
```

```
DialHeight = diameter

PointerWidth = diameter
PointerHeight = diameter / 10
PointerLeft = DialLeft
PointerTop = DialTop + radius - (PointerHeight / 2)

'draw dial and needle
With Worksheets(onsheet).Shapes
    .AddShape(msoShapeOval, DialLeft, DialTop,
DialWidth, DialHeight).Name = "Dial" & gaugename
    .AddShape(msoShapeLeftArrow, PointerLeft,
PointerTop, PointerWidth, PointerHeight).Name =
"Pointer" & gaugename
End With

'draw hashmarks
For Angle = -225 To 45
    rangle = Angle * WorksheetFunction.Pi / 180
    Worksheets(onsheet).Shapes.AddLine centx +
(radius * Cos(rangle)), centy + (radius *
Sin(rangle)), centx + (radius * 0.8 * Cos(rangle)),
centy + (radius * 0.8 * Sin(rangle))
    Angle = Angle + 10
Next Angle

End Function
```

Question 84: External Data: "Where's the code?"

I have an Excel 2003 spreadsheet that retrieves data from an Access database and have it set up to auto-refresh the data on open, three sheets in the workbook are set up to pull data over from separate tables in the database.

Everything is working fine although I had some fun when I wanted to modify the query to bring in some new data ranges in the database. If I modify the query and save it, it wants to add a number to the end of the query name like there are multiple versions of it somewhere.

My question is: Where the heck is the code that does all of this stored in the Excel spreadsheet? I'd like to be able to work directly with it if possible. I know the original query is saved to my C: drive but what about the modified one inside the workbook?

A: Turn on your macro recorder.

Select in the QueryTable resultset. Go to Data/Get External Data/Edit Query; proceed to the QBE Editor.

> File/Return data toe Excel > Turn off the macro recorder.

Alt+F11 toggles between the VB Editor and Sheet. Observe your code. It cna look awful with many Array() elements in the Connection and CommendText, but it can be distilled like this if necessary.

```
CODE
    sSQL = sSQL & "SELECT"
    sSQL = sSQL & "  RC.MFG_SUPERVISOR "

    sSQL = sSQL & "FROM "
    sSQL = sSQL & "  FPRPTSAR.RESPONSIBILITY_CODES_MM
RC "

    With wsData.QueryTables(1)
```

```
        .Connection = Array(Array( _

"ODBC;DSN=DWPROD;;DBQ=DWPROD;DBA=W;APA=T;EXC=F;FEN=T;
QTO=T;FRC=10;FDL=10;LOB=T;RST=T;GDE=F;FRL=F;BAM=IfAll
Successful;MTS=F;MDI=F;CSR=" _
        ), Array("F;FWC=F;PFC=10;TLO=0;"))
        .CommandText = sSQL
        .Refresh BackgroundQuery:=False
    End With
```

The actual code is buried inside an internal procedure.

You can use the Workbook_Open event, for instance.

Modify the Connection string and/or the CommandText string on the fly and execute.

Question 85: Removing the last 2 characters from field

For some reason the text file that I use in Excel has many negative numbers like 37801 - therefore, when I try to add in excel the number is simply skip which is causing all kinds of problems.

Is there away in formula to tell excel to leave off the last 2 characters then multiply by -1?

I tried using =IF(RIGHT(L1,2)=" -",L1-(RIGHT(L1,2)),L1) but all I get is #VALUE (I think because I am trying to subtract a "-" from a number, but not sure how else to do it.

A: Let me see if I have this straight:

You have some negative numbers that are reading in the following format:
  37801 -

And you want to manipulate them, right?

Are they really numbers that are just formatted like that? It sounds like they are not, but to be sure, please try this. In another cell, please type in:

```
=isnumber(L1)
```
(replace A1 with the appropriate cell reference)

Does that return true or false?

Assuming it is FALSE, then I'd recommend the following change to tranpkp's formula:
  =VALUE(IF(RIGHT(L1,2)=" -",LEFT(L1,(LEN(L1)-2))*-1, L1))

The reason being that without wrapping the formula in VALUE, you will still get a text result instead of a number. I also added in *-1 to make the value negative.

Question 86: Chart title

I would like to frame my chart titles (put a box around). Is it possible to do it in Excel?

A: Yes, it is possible. Highlight the title, right click and select "Format Chart Title". Then in the top left hand of the chart title window, select the "automatic" or "custom" options.

Select OK.

It's done!

Question 87: Formula pain

We have a spread sheet to calculate when customers need to come back for their next scheduled oil change. It works really well calculating the mileage versus time and will produce the next date. The problem is when it picks a "Sunday" we would like it to add one day to the date. So, in the cell the formula is in, will display on the screen something like this "Sunday, February 04, 2007"

I tried this formula to see if it could tell there was a Sunday in the cell =IF(D12 ="Sunday"), but only resulted in a FALSE. Not sure why, this operator should see the 'Sunday' in the field.

A: You can do the following:

`=IF((WEEKDAY(A1+17,2))=7,A1+18,A1+17)`

Then, substitute your current calculation for the next appointment date for the red text and be sure to format the column as Date.

Date	Date+17	Next Appt
2/2/2007	2/19/2007	2/19/2007
2/1/2007	2/18/2007	2/19/2007

1/31/2007   2/17/2007   2/17/2007

Or, assuming that your date is in a1...

```
B1: =if(text(a1,"ddd")="Sun",1,0)+a1
```

Question 88: Calculating the number of a type of accident per month

I am trying to improve a monthly report used by a colleague.

Basically the report gives a breakdown of accidents happening within the business throughout the year. There are several different types of accidents.

The spreadsheet is in the following format:

A	B	C	D	E
Date Occurred	Surname	Forename	Description	Month
01/01/07	Blogg	Erl	Slip,trip or Fall	1

There is then a second sheet which summarises the accidents. My colleague wants this sheet revamped so that the totals are calculated automatically instead of manually.

Pivot table.... I hear you all shout

That's what I would normally use for something like this. My problem is is that the first spreadsheet only contains data for 2007 whereas the summary table has to contain data from previous years too. Therefore, in this instance the pivot table option is not really feasible.

I have been looking into using a formula within the summary table. I have tried to use sumproduct, array formulas etc. without success.

A: That's why all data should be stored in one table, and reports should be used to pull out daily, weekly, monthly and even yearly data.

So you should combine all years into one big sheet. They will refer to another worksheet (or workbook, if they prefer) that only shows data from 2007.

Then a Pivot Table can easily be created to display all relevant data!

So where does the summary sheet find the numbers for the previous years and how is that data organised?

You should be able to use SUMIF for it. Maybe a pivot table on multiple consolidation ranges is an option for you if the data for previous years is organised identically to the current year.

Or, an alternative solution is to do it with a PivotTable.

Use EXTERNAL DATA - Excel Files - Your Workbook.

You're going to JOIN the Tables (sheets) containing 2007 and other years in a UNION query

```
CODE
Select *
From Sheet1$
UNION
Select *
Form Sheet2$
```

*Assuming that the columns in all sheets are identical headings.

The query returns a combined resultset and then you Pivot on those results.

Question 89: How to show column titles when scolling down

I have a very long Excel document. When I scroll down (or go to the last record), I lose my column titles. I know there is a way to always show them on the screen, but I cannot find it.

A: Look at the Window Menu - split or freeze panes options.

Click in the cell leftmost and 1 below where your titles are (so if your column title is a1 you would click in b1) and then go to Window, then freeze panes. This will lock your titles in place.

Question 90: Replace *.* by 0

I have an Excel file that comes with strange characters: *.*

I would like to replace these characters by the number 0. I tried with the IF function but it did not work. I guess I did not use it right.

How do I do this correctly?

A: Have *you* tried find and replace using those characters, as it'snot quite as straight-forward as your post would lead the OP to believe?

The problem you have is that Excel treats the asterisk as a wildcard, so you need to cater for that when you do a 'find and replace', and you need to precede the * with a tilde, eg: ~*.* or maybe like this: ~*.~*

Question 91: Excel Macro Help - Copy macro not working

I am trying to create an Excel Macro that will copy data from a CSV file to an XLS file and it is not working. I used the "Record Macro" tool in Excel and the following is what I received.

```
<BEGIN MACRO>
Sub Test1()
'
' Test1 Macro
' Macro recorded 2/8/2007
'
    Range("A1:L46").Select
    Selection.Copy
    Windows("WO_Records.xls").Activate
    Range("A3").Select
    ActiveSheet.Paste
    Application.CutCopyMode = False
    ActiveWorkbook.Save
End Sub
<END MACRO>
```

When I go back into the "WO_Records.xls" file and run the macro, nothing happens. I would like the macro to update the XLS file with the updated data in the CSV file. What am I missing?

A: I'd guess that you didn't activate the CSV after starting the macro recorder when you recorded your macro. The copying appears to start with whatever sheet is active at the time.

Question 92: Excel macro counter

In a training worksheet, data is on lines 14-24. Below macro returns a count of 4 lines (but there are actually 11 lines of data.

```
CODE
Sub LineCnt()

    Cells(14, 1).Select

    Dim r As Integer
    r = 1

    Do While Cells(r, 1).Value <> ""
        r = r + 1
    Loop

    MsgBox ("Lines found: " & r)

End Sub
```

The Excel macro counter does not seem to work.

A: First, Cells(14, 1). Select does nothing for the count.

The cells are counted are from A1 downward until an empty cell is encountered.

A couple of points:

* There is no need to select any cells;
* Your counter is initializing the count at row 1 (r = 1) and counting from there until the first empty cell is found.

Question 93: Launching a macro from a cell

I have given up trying to work this one out for myself. There must be an answer to this somewhere in the Excel Help files, but many days of searching there (and here) have left me with nothing but a dull ache behind my eyes.

Is it possible to launch a macro from a cell? One of my users approached me for a simple change to a macro so that the user could add more lines. Writing the changes to the macro was easy, but I'd like to set it up so that, when the user enters the last cell, she would be given a choice whether or not to add more lines. A "Yes" answer would launch the macro.

If this can't be done (and I'm beginning to believe it can't) I can always give her a command bar button, but it would be neater to automate if possible. Any suggestions?

A: Use the 'Worksheet_SelectionChange' function

```
Private Sub Worksheet._SelectionChange(ByVal Target
As Range)
    If Target.Row = 10 Then 'change 10 to last row of
data
        myresponse = MsgBox("Insert New Row?", _
                    vbYesNo + vbQuestion, "Title")
        If myresponse = vbYes Then
            ActiveCell.Offset(1, 0).Rows.Insert
xlDown
        End If
    End If
End Sub
```

In this sub check whether 'Target' is the last cell, if so, display an msgbox. If result = Yes then insert new row.

Question 94: Font formatting inside a comment box

I was wondering if anyone knew how to format text (e.g. make bold) within a comment box in Excel using VBA. I want to make certain portions of the text bold.

It's easy to do manually, but with the "Macro recorder" it doesn't write any code for the formatting.

Unlike the 'cells' member, the 'comments' member doesn't have a 'characters' property to allow one to format part of the text.

How can I do this right?

A: You need to access the comment as a shape. For example:

```
Dim myCom As Comment
Set myCom = ActiveCell.AddComment
myCom.Text "Hello This is my comment right here"
myCom.Shape.TextFrame.Characters(1, 10).Font.Bold
= True
```

With 1 being the first character you want Bold and 10 being the length you want to make bold.

Question 95: VBA to copy text from two separate text boxes

I am trying to figure out how to copy the text that is contained in two different text boxes in an excel sheet and combine and concatenate that text into a third textbox on a different sheet in the same workbook.

Are there any quick code ideas?

A: Try it like this:

```
Worksheets("sheet2name").TextBoxName =
Worksheets("sheet1name").TextBox1Name &
Worksheets("sheet1name").TextBox2Name
```

Question 96: Listing Excel Files in a New Excel File

I have a directory with 100 Excel files in it (let's call it c:\data). I want to write a macro (in a separate file) which creates a list of all the files in the directory c:\data in column A.

Thus if the files in C:\data were RHH100.xls RHH203.xls and RHH675.xls, my macro (in file C:\control\master.xls) would run and then Column A in Sheet 1 would have the three file names in it.

How can I do this?

A: In Visual Basic Editor set a reference to 'Microsoft Scripting Runtime' by going to Tools, References and ticking the box.

Paste the following into a module:

```
Dim fso As Scripting.FileSystemObject
Dim fldr As Folder, fl As File
Dim lngRow As Long
Set fso =
CreateObject("Scripting.FileSystemObject")
    Set fldr = fso.GetFolder("C:\")
    lngRow = 0
    For Each fl In fldr.Files
        lngRow = lngRow + 1
        Cells(lngRow, 1).FormulaR1C1 = fl.Path
    Next
    set fso = nothing
```

There is another way of doing it without external references:

```
CODE
Const cDir = "\path\to\dir\"
Dim strName As String
Dim lngRow As Long
lngRow = 0
strName = Dir(cDir & "*.xls")
While strName <> ""
  lngRow = lngRow + 1
```

```
Cells(lngRow, 1).Value = cDir & strName
  strName = Dir()
Wend
```

Question 97: Trouble with Excel VB code move from row to row

I have about 50+ rows of excel data of a length from A thru F. I want to copy each row one at a time to say r30 to w30, perform some if/then statements that are working for me, and then print a sheet2 which has a lot of text boxes and labels that reference to r30 to w30 that create a label. After it has printed the sheet2 with the copied data from r30 to w30, I want to clear the data form r30 to w30 and start over but have the selected cells be the next row down that has data past the orginal 1st row. So if I started with my data rows at sheet1.Range("A12:F12"), how do I get a code that will move me to the next row that has data in it. I can do the code for the copy, paste, clear cells, print sheet but cannot figure a way to have it move down the rows or loop. I could write code for each row but each time I open the Sheet1, the rows can be anywhere from 2 rows of data to 200 rows of data and I need a seperate printout for each row.

How can I accomplish this?

A: You need to do some reading to get up to speed on the Excel Object Model. For now, you can do as follows:

```
CODE
dim r as range
for each r in range([A12], [A12].end(xldown))
  range(r, r.offset(0,5)).copy [r30]
  'now do the other stuff
next
```

The macro recorder is your friend. Record, observe, play around with modifying code. Tinker. Try things out. Ask questions.

Question 98: Populating second column of list box

I have a form with a listbox which is populated with the names of sheets in my workbook. I want to have 2 columns, the first is the sheet name and the second will be the value of a cell on that sheet. This is the code I currently have:

```
CODE
Private Sub UserForm_Initialize()
    Dim wbs As Worksheet

    For Each wbs In Worksheets
        If wbs.Name <> "Contents" Then
        If wbs.Name <> "Status" Then
        If wbs.Name <> "Introduction" Then
        If wbs.Name <> "Template" Then
        If wbs.Range("G10") > 0 Then
            ListBox1.ColumnCount = 2
            ListBox1.AddItem wbs.Name, 0
            ListBox1.AddItem wbs.Range("D4"), 1

        End If
        End If
        End If
        End If
        End If
    Next

End Sub
```

This doesn't work because the sheet name and the cell contents are showing on different lines on the list in the first column.

Is it possible for me to get the sheet name in the first and the cell contents in the second column?

A: You may try this:
```
...
ListBox1.AddItem wbs.Name
ListBox1.Column(1, ListBox1.ListCount - 1) =
wbs.Range("D4").Value
```

...

Question 99: Automatic Conditioning of Text Cell Entries

I'm using Microsoft Excel 2003 and am trying to achieve the following:

* A user enters text into a cell

* Excel will automatically format the cell into Title Case

Simple what I want to achieve, but it's proving harder than I thought it'd be!

Also, does anyone believe this can be achieved without VB?

One last question though - is it possible to format the text as Title Case instead of UPPERCASE (MR JOE BLOGGS)?

A: Copy this code and paste into the SHEET OBJECT Code Window.

```
CODE
Private Sub Worksheet_Change(ByVal Target As Range)
    If Target.Count > 1 Then Exit Sub
    If Not Intersect(Target, Range("A1:A10")) Is
Nothing Then
        Target.Value = UCase(Target.Value)
    End If
End Sub
```

Obviously, the RANGE will need to be your intended range.

Also this code anticipates single cell entries, not copy 'n' paste.

On your second question, VB has no such function. However, Excel does.

```
CODE
    Target.Value = Application.Proper(Target.Value)
```

Question 100: Find certain cells based on text colour

I have a list of text in a column. Some of these text values are in red colour.

I would like to identify these cells that have text in red, by putting a "1" in the adjacent cell.

Is this possible?

A: You need a loop to go through your list and where the returned color is red then make the next row / column = 1

```
CODE
isred = 123  ' What ever color red is

if IsRed = Cells(x, y).Interior.Color then
    'make next cell equal 1
    Cells(x, y +1).value = 1
end if
```

You can also try something along the lines of:

```
CODE
Sub see_red()
For Each cll In Selection
    If cll.Font.ColorIndex = 3 Then
        cll.Offset(0, 1) = 1
    End If
Next cll
End Sub
```

Highlight the column or the cells you want to check and then run the macro.

I find it easiest to use the macro recorder when performing the desired action (here, turning certain cells red) and then modifying the code.

Question 101: Data Validation List to Select Worksheet in Macro

I have a Data Validation list in cell A1 of a worksheet called LIST.

I would like to modify the macro that I have recorded; the macro uses data from various worksheets. I would like to sort out some code so that at certain points in the macro it will select the worksheet that is shown in cell A1 of the LIST sheet and then carry out the code already recorded.

This will allow me to quickly change a sheet name that is refererred to in the macro numerous times without actually manually editing the sheet name in the macro code.

I have highlighted in red the three times during my macro that I need the code to refer to whatever sheet name appears in cell C2 of the worksheet named LIST.

```
Sub METASTOCK2()
```

A: This is a starting a starting point:

```
Dim strSheet As String
strSheet = Sheets("LIST").Range("C2").Value
Sheets(strSheet).Select 'Sheets("BRENT CRUDE").Select
...
```

This will do exactly what you want.

Question 102: Get cell value from external file

I have a series of Daily planner files that I am opening and copying the value of specific cells ($K$49 in this case represents # of hours worked) into a spreadsheet for comparison and analysis.

When I use the following snippet of code the first example puts the formula in the cell which results in data, but when I use Sum() on the hours shown I get a total of Zero. The 2nd example results in Error 2023.

How can I fix this?

A: Instead of "evaluate", why not use ".value"?
Also, you've defined "WorkbookName" but not "WorbookName1".

See the following examples:

```
----------------Example 1-------------------------
WorkbookName = "='" & Mid(Filename, 1, X - 1) & "[" &
_
Mid(Filename, X, Len(Filename) - X + 1) & "]Charlie'"
Filename_Intime = WorkbookName & "!$K$49"
. . .
Range(Cells(DP_Row, Col_In), Cells(DP_Row,
Col_In)).Formula = Filename_Intime

Results from Watch:
WorkbookName = "='G:\Cmills\Excel\Daily
Planners\2004\May 2004\[Daily Planner 2004-05-
14.xls]Charlie'"

Filename_Intime = "='G:\Cmills\Excel\Daily
Planners\2004\May 2004\[Daily Planner 2004-05-
14.xls]Charlie'!$K$49"
```

```
----------------Example 2-------------------------
WorkbookName = "'" & Mid(Filename, 1, X - 1) & "[" &
_
Mid(Filename, X, Len(Filename) - X + 1) &
"]Charlie'!$K$49"
Filename_Intime = Evaluate(WorkbookName1)
...
Range(Cells(DP_Row, Col_In), Cells(DP_Row,
Col_In)).Value = Filename_Intime

Results from Watch:
WorkbookName = "'G:\Cmills\Excel\Daily
Planners\2004\May 2004\[Daily Planner 2004-05-
14.xls]Charlie!'$K$49"

Filename_Intime : Error 2023
```

What about this (in example 1)?

```
With Range(Cells(DP_Row, Col_In), Cells(DP_Row,
Col_In))
   .Formula = Filename_Intime
   .Value = Val(.Value)
End
```

Question 103: Excel Text box Formatting

I have a worksheet with some text boxes on it for user input. I am trying to set up a format so that when the user inputs a number, it shows as a percentage, i.e., user enters 30, and text box shows 30%.

I have used some VB to set other text boxes to show $ for currency fields, but I cannot seem to get it to work for percentages.

Here is the code I used for the dollar sign:

```
TextBox13.Value = Format(TextBox13.Value,
"$#,##0")
```

I tried to use this:

```
TextBox51.Value = Format(Val(TextBox51.Value) /
100, "##%")
```

This ended up giving me the percent sign, right as soon as a number was entered. If I needed to type 65, it would show 6% and not take the 5. The cursor defaults to after the % and I manually have to back up to make the text box read 65%.

A: I assume you have your code in the textbox's change event.

```
CODE
Private Sub TextBox1_Change()
TextBox1.Value = Format(Val(TextBox1.Value) / 100,
"##%")
TextBox1.SelStart = Len(TextBox1.Value) - 1
End Sub
```

Question 104: Prevent leaving cell blank (empty)

How can I prevent a user from leaving a cell blank (empty)?

I would like column A to not allow any blank cells. I am trying to prevent the end user from entering data into a cell if there are any empty cells above it.

A: Try this:

```
CODE
Private Sub Worksheet_SelectionChange(ByVal Target As
Range)
    Dim curr_row As Long, curr_col As Long, prev_row
As Long

    curr_row = Selection.Row
    curr_col = Selection.Column
    prev_row = curr_row - 1

    If prev_row > 0 And curr_col = 1 Then
        If Trim(Cells(prev_row, 1)) = "" Then
            MsgBox ("Please enter a value in the
previous cell")
            Cells(prev_row, 1).Select
        End If
    End If
End Sub
```

Or this:

```
CODE
Private Sub Worksheet_SelectionChange(ByVal Target As
Range)
    With Target
        If .Column <> 1 Then Exit Sub
        If .Row > 1 Then
            With .Offset(-1)
                If .Value = "" Then .Select
            End With
        End If
    End With
End Sub
```

Right click the sheet tab, select, Vide Code and paste into the Code Window.

It already is set up to work on the FIRST column.

Question 105: Excel formulae count

I have searched my books and the net to find out if there is a formulae collection in Excel. I feel there must be but cannot find any info.

I have some code that performs a Selection.SpecialCells(xlCellTypeFormulas, 23). Select but if there are no formulae an error occurs. I have put an on error condition in place to avoid the problem but I think it would be cleaner if I could establish whether there are any formulae present before launching into my logic.

Any ideas would be welcome.

A: There is nothing wrong with using error trapping for this

The only other way I can think of doing this would be to use the FIND method looking in formulae and checking for "=" but that may find things that have an "=" in the middle of some text so isn't particularly robust - personmally, I would use error trapping - that's what it is there for.

Please read FAQ222-2244.

Also, take a look at the HasFormula Property.

Question 106: Insert data in Excel 2003 cells from Access 2003

I have a template that I want to preserve. I want to open it and save is as another every time. But there does not seem to be a SaveAs option. Then I thought I would open it, save it as something else. This does work when I open the new document. It opens the template again.

Here is what I have so far.

```
CODE
Dim oApp As Object
    Dim SheetName As String
    Set oApp = CreateObject("Excel.Application")

    'load document
    oApp.Workbooks.Open ("C:\AirMonitoring\Work Area
Air Sampling Log.xls")

    ' save as new document
    SheetName =
"C:\AirMonitoring\Spreadsheets\WorkAreaAirSamplingLog
-" & Me.Project_Number & ".xls"
    oApp.Save (SheetName)

    'close template
    oApp.Workbooks.Close

    ' open new one back up
    oApp.Workbooks.Open (SheetName)

    ' make Excel visible
    oApp.Visible = True
```

A: First, save your template as a template (*.xlt).

Then use the Add method of the Workbooks collection (instead of Open):

```
Dim oApp As Object
Dim SheetName As String
Set oApp = CreateObject("Excel.Application")
```

```
'load NEW document
oApp.Workbooks.Add "C:\AirMonitoring\Work Area Air
Sampling Log.xlt"
' save as new document
SheetName =
"C:\AirMonitoring\Spreadsheets\WorkAreaAirSamplingLog
-" & Me.Project_Number & ".xls"
oApp.ActiveWorkbook.SaveAs SheetName
' make Excel visible
oApp.Visible = True
```

Question 107: Control Word from Excel with VBA

I am in the process of creating an Excel macro that takes values from a spreadsheet and creates a word document. I am practically done with the project but I can not get around one error when creating a shape in Word. I have created a small macro for troubleshooting wich is pasted here. I get "Object variable or with block not set on the sh = appWD.ActiveDocument... line.

The same code minus "appWD." works fine in a Word macro.

```
Sub Test3()

Dim appWD As Word.Application

    ' Create a new instance of Word & make it visible
        Set appWD =
CreateObject("Word.Application.8")

        With appWD
            .Visible = True
            .Activate
            .WindowState = wdWindowStateNormal
         End With

        appWD.ScreenUpdating = True

        ' Tell Word to create a new document
        appWD.Documents.Add
```

```
        'Draw Rectangle
        Dim sh As Shape

        sh =
appWD.ActiveDocument.Shapes.AddShape(msoShapeRectangl
e, Left:=90, Top:=70, Width:=72, Height:=72)

    End Sub
```

A: Try this:

```
sh = appWD.ActiveDocument.Shapes.AddShape(1,
Left:=90, Top:=70, Width:=72, Height:=72) '
1=msoShapeRectangle
```

Don't forget it's an OBJECT:

CODE

```
Set sh =
appWD.ActiveDocument.Shapes.AddShape(msoShapeRectangl
e, Left:=90, Top:=70, Width:=72, Height:=72)
```

You may also want to explicitly declare it as:

CODE
```
Dim sh As Word.Shape
The code may think of it as an Excel Shape.  I know
this often happens with people declaring:

Dim rng As Range
```

When they are controlling stuff in Word, from Excel. If not explicitly declared as a Word Range, an Excel macro will assume (correctly) that Range means an Excel range. They are very different beasties. Not sure if this would apply to Shape, but if you can declare it explicitly as a Word Shape, it may be better to do so.

Question 108: Dynamic Values in Excel Chart

I'm trying to assign variables as dynamic coordinates in ActiveChart object. However, I keep 'Application Defined or Object Defined Error' Typing "F2:F30" does work. How can I keep this dynamic?

```
Set Rng1 = Range("F" & i, Range("F" & i + 77))
Set Rng2 = Range("X" & i, "X" & (i + 77))
Set Rng3 = Range(Rng1, Rng2)


   Charts.Add
    ActiveChart.ChartType = xlLine
    ActiveChart.SetSourceData
Source:=Sheets("5_Min").Range ("Rng1", "Rng2"),
PlotBy:=xlRows
    ActiveChart.SeriesCollection(1).XValues =
Sheets("5_Min").Range("Rng2")
```

A: You do not really need code to do this.

How can I rename a table as it changes size FAQ68-1331?

So if your range name is WeekOf, then in your Chart/Source/Series Tab - WhateverSheetName!WeekOf for each Value/Caregory.

You mix objects, addresses and strings:
- the first three lines set Rng1 and Rng2 as ranges in active sheet, Rng3 as a range Fi:Xi+77,
- in two last lines you yse hard strings "Rng1" and "Rng2", that have nothing to do with initially set ranges.

If you want to work with strings, use:
Rng1 = "F" & i &":F" & i + 77
...
Rng3 = "F" & i &":X" & i + 77
(if necessary, Trim it) and next:

ActiveChart.SetSourceData Source:=Sheets("5_Min").Range (Rng3), PlotBy:=xlRows

Or when using ranges:
Set Rng3=Sheets("5_Min").Range("F" & i &":X" & i + 77)
...
ActiveChart.SetSourceData Source:=Rng3, PlotBy:=xlRows

Question 109: Generate filename from 4 different cells

I'm almost there. The last thing that has me stymied is generating a filename, with a loop.

I have a function that loops through a set of values on sheet 1, plugs them into sheet 2, performs calculations, and then saves the workbook, and then goes to the next set of values, lather, rinse, and repeat.

I'd like to generate the filename dynamically, which would save us the trouble of editing the values list every month. It will have about 50 lines, when all is said and done.

What I want is a filename in the format FEB07AUD5061. This is broken down as follows:

FEB - this is Sheet2!G4 converted to a month. Sheet2!G4 has a single number in it. So for this example, it would say "2".

07 - this is the last two digits of Sheet2!G2 - which in this case says "2007"

AUD - this is the first three characters of the item in my value list in column A, sheet 1.

5061 - This is the value in col c, sheet 1.

So for the following values:

```
COL A    B    C
Alpha    00001  510
Alpha    00001  520
Alpha    00001  540
Bravo    00001  560
Bravo    00001  590
```

I would like to generate the following file names, for example:

FEB07ALP510
FEB07ALP520
FEB07ALP540
FEB07BRA560
FEB07BRA590

Here's my code:

```
CODE
Private Sub CmdRunSpreadsheet_Click()
'
'
' To insert values and create monthly budget
distribution automatically

'Check for login to spreadsheet server
    If MsgBox("Are you logged in to Spreadsheet
Server?", vbYesNo, "Login") = vbNo Then
    Exit Sub
    Else
```

'1. Unhide button, and all worksheets and rows

```
    cmdRunSpreadsheet.Visible = True
    Sheets("GXE Source").Visible = True
    Sheets("DistList").Visible = True

    Rows("1:8").Select
    Range("A8").Activate
    Selection.EntireRow.Hidden = False
    Columns("A:E").Select
    Range("A9").Activate
    Selection.EntireColumn.Hidden = False
```

'2. Get values from Master Sheet

```
    Dim r As Range
    For Each r In
Sheets("DistList").Range(Sheets("DistList").[A1],
Sheets("DistList").[A1].End(xlDown))
        sDept = r.Value
        nVal1 = r.Offset(0, 1).Value
        nVal2 = r.Offset(0, 2).Value
        sName = r.Offset(0, 3).Value
    'BudgetStatus is where the processing occurs
        With Sheets("BudgetStatus")
```

```
'.Cells(10, "A").Value = sDept
.Cells(6, "G").Value = nVal1
.Cells(7, "G").Value = nVal2
End With
```

'3. Calculate

```
Application.Calculate
```

'4. Generate Detail Reports, and hide GXE sheet
```
Application.Run ("ExpandDetailReports")
```

'5. Hide all extraneous rows on worksheet

```
Rows("1:8").Select
Range("A8").Activate
Selection.EntireRow.Hidden = True
Columns("A:E").Select
Range("A9").Activate
Selection.EntireColumn.Hidden = True
```

'6. Hide button, GXE sheet, and master values sheet.

```
cmdRunSpreadsheet.Visible = False
Sheets("GXE Source").Visible = False
Sheets("DistList").Visible = False
```

'7. Overwrite formulae with values, confirm first

```
        If MsgBox("Do you want to convert all
formulas?", vbYesNo, "Remove Formulas?") = vbNo Then

    Exit Sub
        Else


        Cells.Select
        Range("A38").Activate
        Selection.Copy
        Selection.PasteSpecial Paste:=xlValues,
Operation:=xlNone, SkipBlanks:= _
            False, Transpose:=False
        ActiveWindow.ScrollRow = 1


        End If
```

149

```
SaveAs "C:\Documents and
Settings\Administrator\Desktop" & "\" & sName &
".xls"
```

```
Next
```

```
End If
```

```
End Sub
```

Currently, in the saveas section, sName refers to a hardcoded filename on the values list on sheet1. This would have to change every month manually in order to prevent the recipients of the workbook overwriting their report every month.

I did create a cell on sheet 1 with =DATE(BudgetStatus!G2,BudgetStatus!G4,1) in it, (where BudgetStatus is sheet 2), which gives me the correct month in mmm format. I tried concatenate in another cell to just get it to read "FEB07", where BudgetStatus!G2 says "2007" but it just gives me the excel date for FEB. So i'm just thinking it would be easier to generate the filename in VBA anyway.

A: Something like this should do it:

```
With Sheets("BudgetStatus")
   sName = UCase(Format(DateSerial(.[G2], .[G4], 1),
"mmmyy") & Left(sDept, 3)) & nVal2
End With
```

Question 110: Accessing a proprietary toolbar in Excel

I've been working on a module in excel to run some procedures using an add-in we purchased for Excel called Spreadsheet Server. This program adds a toolbar to Excel. I need to figure out how to 'push' a button on that toolbar using VBA. Recording a macro of it doesn't work - I get an empty module. Same goes for recording a macro accessing the Spreadsheet Server Menu item on my main Excel menu.

The menu item is two to the right of the Help menu item - after the Adobe PDF menu item.

How can I resolve this?

I actually contacted the manufacturer, and he said I can run that using this:

Application.Run ("ExpandDetailReports")

I haven't tested it yet. I'm stuck on the fact that Calculate is only calculating my one main sheet, and not all the sheets in the workbook.

For the record, it is listed as "SServer - for JDE". It was not checked. Is there something I need to do (check it for example) to make it available in VBA?

A: Yes, check it in the References. The open the Object Browser and browse ONLY that reference's objects to determine if they might include the toolbar objects or anything else that might be useful.

Question 111: Converting a string to an array of integers

Is there an easy way in vba to convert a string to an array of integers? For example:

I have this particular array of numbers in the element <column_data_types> in a xml file:

<column_data_types>1, 1, 1, 1, 1, 1, 1, 1, 1, 5, 5, 5, 1, 1, 1</column_data_types>

I have a function that will grab the array of numbers but the function returns a string. ("1, 1, 1, 1, 1, 1, 1, 1, 1, 5, 5, 5, 1, 1, 1") For this particular situation I actually need this list of numbers to be numbers, not a string, and pass them to an array in excel? Below is the situation that I'm talking about; I am importing a query from a database and need to fill out the .TextFileColumnDataTypes argument which takes an array of integers. I need this to be dynamic so I put these columndatatypes in an xml file.

```
    With
WorkSheet("x").QueryTables.Add(Connection:="TEXT;" &
ExcelFilePath & "\FABRICREQ",
Destination:=Range("FD_StartData"))
        .Name = "FabricData"
        .FieldNames = True
        .RowNumbers = False
        .FillAdjacentFormulas = False
        .PreserveFormatting = True
        .RefreshOnFileOpen = False
        .RefreshStyle = xlInsertDeleteCells
        .SavePassword = False
        .SaveData = True
        .AdjustColumnWidth = False
        .RefreshPeriod = 0
        .TextFilePromptOnRefresh = False
        .TextFilePlatform = 437
        .TextFileStartRow = 1
        .TextFileParseType = xlDelimited
        .TextFileTextQualifier =
xlTextQualifierDoubleQuote
```

```
    .TextFileConsecutiveDelimiter = False
    .TextFileTabDelimiter = False
    .TextFileSemicolonDelimiter = False
    .TextFileCommaDelimiter = True
    .TextFileSpaceDelimiter = False
    .TextFileColumnDataTypes = Array(1, 1, 1, 1,
1, 1, 1, 1, 1, 5, 5, 5, 1, 1, 1)
    .TextFileTrailingMinusNumbers = True
    .Refresh BackgroundQuery:=False
  End With
```

Instead of looking like the above: .TextFileColumnDataTypes = Array(1, 1, 1, 1, 1, 1, 1, 1, 1, 5, 5, 5, 1, 1, 1)

It will look like this: .TextFileColumnDataTypes = Array(getXmlValue) except getXmlValue returns a string which is the problem.

How I should handle this?

A: One way to do it would be:

CODE
```
    a = Split(getXmlValue, ",")
    ReDim b(UBound(a))
    For i = 0 To UBound(a)
        b(i) = Int(a(i))
    Next
```

153

Question 112: Loop through 3 columns to get values

I'm working on a bit of code to loop through values on one worksheet, and enter them into another worksheet. This is part of a larger function that will then save each set of values off in a separate worksheet. Right now, I'm just trying to get the loop to work, so i'm using a message box to watch it.

My values on Sheet 1 are:

Alpha   00001   510   FEB07MER510
Bravo   00001   520   FEB07MER520
Charlie   00001   540   FEB07MER540
Delta   00001   560   FEB07MER560
Echo   00001   590   FEB07MER590
Foxtrot   00001   3300   FEB07MER3300
Golf   00001   3310   FEB07MER3310
Hotel   00001   3320   FEB07MER3320
India   00001   2600   FEB07MER2600
Juliet   00001   2620   FEB07MER2620

Right now, my code is:

CODE

```
Dim r As Range
For Each r In
Sheets("DistList").Range(Sheets("DistList").[A1],
Sheets("DistList").[A1].End(xlDown))
   sDept = r.Value
   nVal1 = r.Offset(0.1).Value
   nVal2 = r.Offset(0.2).Value
   sName = r.Offset(0.3).Value
MsgBox nVal2
```

I'm using this to troubleshoot this module, in which I have code which takes the values in colums A:D and plugs them into my other spreadsheet and then saves each one as a separate workbook. In the above example, I cannot make the nval, nval2, and sName return the right things. They should return the values in the columns B, C, and D, respectively. Right now, as written, the msgbox loops through the values in column A, instead of column C.

Any suggestions?

A: Try this:

```
nVal1 = r.Offset(0, 1).Value
```

INDEX

.

www.ingramcontent.com/pod-product-compliance
Lightning Source LLC
Chambersburg PA
CBHW051053050326
40690CB00006B/709